A SPLASH OF CITRUS

RECIPES FROM THE JUNIOR LEAGUE OF GREATER WINTER HAVEN

MISSION

The Junior League of Greater Winter Haven, Inc., is an organization of women committed to promoting voluntarism, developing the potential of women, and improving the community through the effective action and leadership of trained volunteers. Its purpose is exclusively educational and charitable.

THE JUNIOR LEAGUE OF GREATER WINTER HAVEN
Women building better communities

A SPLASH OF CITRUS

RECIPES FROM THE JUNIOR LEAGUE OF GREATER WINTER HAVEN

Copyright © 2013 by
Junior League of Greater Winter Haven
P.O. Box 7161
Winter Haven, Florida 33883-7161
863-583-7659

Photography © by C. Michael Potthast
Potthast Studios

Published by

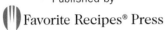 Favorite Recipes® Press

An imprint of

 SOUTHWESTERN
Publishing Group®

P.O. Box 305142
Nashville, Tennessee 37230
1-800-358-0560

Library of Congress Control Number: 2013946496
ISBN: 978-0-87197-591-1

Publisher and President: Dave Kempf
Editorial Director: Mary Cummings
Art Direction and Design: Steve Newman
Project Editor: Tanis Westbrook

This cookbook is a collection of favorite recipes,
which are not necessarily original recipes.

Printed in the United States of America
First Printing: 2013
5,000 copies

A Splash of Citrus

Recipes from the Junior League of Greater Winter Haven

FOREWORD

fla·vor (n): a distinctive taste, atmosphere, or quality

Welcome to the Junior League of Greater Winter Haven's *A Splash of Citrus*, a unique cookbook that captures the heart and soul of Central Florida's Polk County and the culinary talents of the people who truly epitomize the definition of real Florida flavor. Florida produces more oranges than any other region of the world, except Brazil, and leads the world in grapefruit production. Polk County is Florida's largest citrus producer, with the citrus industry playing an important role in our culture, heritage, economy, and the everyday life of our citizens and our visitors. In fact, the citrus industry generates more than $9 billion in economic activity in Florida annually.

According to the Florida Department of Citrus, most oranges bloom in March and April, with early varieties, such as Hamlins and Parson Browns, reaching maturity from October through January. "Mid-season" varieties such as the Pineapple Orange reach maturity from December through February. "Late season" varieties, including the popular Valencia, mature from March through June. All citrus, including oranges, must ripen on the tree, as citrus does not ripen once it is picked. Ultimately, the sugar to acid ratio will determine the flavor of juice, all of which must meet exacting standards in order to be sold as 100% Florida orange juice.

However, dining in Central Florida's Polk County is more than just eating—it's an experience. Among the many things to do in Central Florida, Polk County also provides travelers an ideal destination to indulge in exceptional dining experiences. Feast on slow-roasted barbecue at a restaurant decorated with antique farm tools, head to a rustic fish camp for an old-fashioned fish fry, or indulge in a six-course meal served in one of our numerous historic dining rooms. Fish is a local favorite here, but you'll also find food from around the globe.

From alligator tail and oysters to flame-broiled steak, fresh seafood, and other famous southern fare like mouthwatering barbecue, Central Florida's Polk County is a sizzling smorgasbord of culinary pleasures.

You will find this amazing flavor not only throughout *A Splash of Citrus*, but also in many of our favorite local dining spots, where each restaurant provides a unique dining atmosphere that can range from funky to elegant. You will also find these same flavors (and many more) in our homes and on our tables each and every day. That's the essence of this inspiring new cookbook. We hope that you enjoy these recipes and that you will come to visit us to experience all the flavors that Central Florida's Polk County has to offer. For those times that you can't quite make it here, it is our hope that you will enjoy this unique and exquisite collection of authentic Central Florida recipes, and that in some small way experiencing these flavors, wherever you may be, will transport you here, if just for a little while. Enjoy the flavors of Central Florida's Polk County. We hope to see you soon in Sunny Central Florida!

With our very warmest regards—enjoy!!!

Visit Central Florida
www.visitcentralflorida.org

PREFACE

The pages of this cookbook contain more than just recipes — they contain memories and history, all from a very special place located in the heart of the Sunshine State. This collection of recipes reflects the essence of what the Greater Winter Haven area means to those who call it home. There are ice-cold cocktails to enjoy on a hot day spent splashing in the Chain of Lakes, fresh seafood to dine on after a vacation to the beach, and desserts laced with the sweetness of orange blossoms on a sunny afternoon.

While our beautiful blue lakes and lush green citrus groves define our landscape and our heritage, the heart of our area lies with its people. We're a mix of lifelong residents, newcomers, and those who grew up here, moved away, and then returned to put down roots in this wonderful community. It's this mix of people the Junior League of Greater Winter Haven strives to serve through a wide variety of community projects.

Since 1981, Junior League women have launched the Women's Resource Center, established the Winter Haven Public Library's Young Readers' Room and the Regency Center for Women's Neonatal Family Room, and promoted healthy families through projects like Family Fit Fest and Kids in the Kitchen. The Junior League also supports education and literacy.

None of this would be possible without the tireless hours logged by our members, coupled with the generosity of local businesses and individuals who support our fund-raisers. The funding support of our community is the driving force behind every project. *A Splash of Citrus* is yet another means of funding our community projects, and we appreciate your support of the Junior League of Greater Winter Haven and its mission.

We hope that our freshly picked recipes will quickly become your favorites, giving you a taste of the Greater Winter Haven area and helping you create memories for years to come.

A Splash of Citrus Cookbook Committee

SPONSORS

ORANGE

GRAPEFRUIT

TANGERINE

Ginny's Creative Design

Noble Juice

Applied Aquatic Management

LEMON

Arabellas

Publix

BLUEBERRY

Grape Expectations   Harry's Old Place

Pro Med Healthcare Services   Sweet Magnolia's Tea Bistro

Dr. & Mrs. Stephen Beissinger   Amy P. Tucker, P.L., Attorney at Law

DR. MARY B. JEWITT

Dr. Jewett paved the way for women in our community.

Dr. Mary B. Jewett, a spirited woman, arrived in Winter Haven in 1910 or 1911 to assist her sister, Mrs. F. W. Inman, after the death of her husband. Dr. Jewett quickly succumbed to the beauty of Winter Haven's natural landscape and even invested in citrus groves. As a practicing physician, Dr. Jewett was an inspiration to many young women, as female doctors were a rarity during that time.

Dr. Jewett's energy and enthusiasm were contagious, and she was not in Winter Haven long before she formed a group whose mission was to improve the city. The first meeting was held on November 18, 1913. At the inaugural gathering, sixty-four women signed the constitution and enrolled as charter members. The organization became known as "the Woman's Civic League," and the women took on many tasks, such as creating a city park, improving the downtown area, and expanding the library. At the time, the "library" consisted of a few books in the local drugstore.

Dr. Jewett paved the way for women in our community. Today, the Junior League of Greater Winter Haven, Inc., carries on the traditions and values established by Dr. Jewett. It remains an organization of women committed to promoting voluntarism, developing the potential of women, and improving the community through the effective action and leadership of trained volunteers. Its purpose is exclusively educational and charitable.

SAINT FIACRE
PATRON SAINT OF THE GARDENERS
PLACED HERE IN APPRECIATION OF THE SERVICES
OF OUR VERNON RUTTER, SR., SUPT.

Contents

COCKTAILS & APPETIZERS

CITRUS

A century ago the community of Winter Haven was known not only for its warm weather but also for the delicious Florida citrus grown in the heart of the Sunshine State. Families began planting groves of tangerines, oranges, grapefruit, lemons, and limes, and soon a glass of 100% Florida orange juice became a staple on breakfast tables across the country. The citrus industry continues to be a proud family tradition with several generations working together in the groves and packinghouses to cultivate the land and bring modern-day technology to the original 1920s packinghouses built by an earlier generation.

Winter Haven was home to the Florida Citrus Showcase, originally known as the Florida Orange Festival, for eighty-four years. The Showcase was an exposition with citrus contests, a queen contest, and a coronation ball. Many television crews came to Winter Haven for exposition week, putting Winter Haven on national broadcast television annually. Many old-timers recall with nostalgia the beautiful, artistic exhibits that carried out an "Alice in Citrusland" theme and other fairy tales. It seemed appropriate because the citrus industry has provided a fairyland of wealth to Florida and this area of the state, especially many Winter Haven citizens.

TANGERINE PARADISE

Serves 1

2 ounces Noble™ 100% pure tangerine guava mango juice
1 ounce coconut-flavored rum

Mix the juice and rum in a small pitcher and pour into a martini glass. You may substitute tangerine juice for the tangerine guava mango juice.

THREE-FROG PIÑA COLADAS

Serves 6

1 1/2 cups rum
1 cup cream of coconut
4 cups cubed fresh pineapple
2 tablespoons fresh lime juice
1/2 cup milk
1/3 cup shredded coconut
Ice

Add the rum, cream of coconut, pineapple, lime juice, milk and coconut to a blender container. Fill with ice and process to desired consistency, adding additional ice if needed. Serve in chilled glasses.

BLONDE SANGRIA

Serves 8

1 (750-ml) bottle chardonnay or
   pinot grigio
1 1/4 cups pineapple juice
1 cup lemon-lime soda
1/3 cup orange juice
1/4 cup sugar

2 tablespoons fresh lemon juice
1 tablespoon fresh lime juice
Crushed ice
1/2 cup raspberries
1/2 cup finely chopped apple

Combine the wine, pineapple juice, soda, orange juice, sugar, lemon juice and lime juice in a pitcher and stir until the sugar is dissolved. Fill wine glasses one-half full with crushed ice and add a few raspberries and apple pieces to each glass. Pour the sangria into the glasses and serve.

CITRUS SANGRIA

Serves 6

1 (750-ml) bottle dry red wine
3/4 cup sugar
2 cups club soda
4 1/2 teaspoons Grand Marnier
1 large orange
1 large lemon

Combine the wine, sugar, club soda and Grand Marnier in a pitcher and stir until the sugar is dissolved. Cut the orange and lemon in half and squeeze the juice from one orange half and one lemon half into the pitcher. Cut the remaining orange half and lemon half into thin slices and add to the pitcher. Chill for a few hours to overnight. Serve over ice.

Brazilian Caipirinha

Serves 1

1 lime
1 tablespoon cane sugar or 2 tablespoons simple syrup
Crushed ice
2 ounces Brazilian cachaça

Cut the lime into eighths and add to an old-fashioned glass. Add the sugar and crush the lime and sugar with a pestle. Add crushed ice and cachaça and stir.

Variation

Try this drink with fresh tangerine, lime, lemon, passion fruit, pineapple, or your favorite fruit, or mix several of the fruits together.

Frozen Margaritas

Serves 8

12 ounces frozen limeade concentrate
1 1/2 cups fresh orange juice
3/4 cup tequila
3/4 cup Grand Marnier

Crushed ice
Additional Grand Marnier
Margarita salt

Add the limeade concentrate, orange juice, tequila and 3/4 cup Grand Marnier to a blender container. Fill with ice. Process to desired consistency, adding additional ice if needed. Dip the rim of margarita glasses in Grand Marnier and then into salt to coat. Pour the margaritas into the prepared glasses and enjoy.

Skinny Mixed Berry Margaritas

Serves 4

16 ounces strawberries
3 ounces raspberries
3 ounces blackberries
6 ounces blueberries
Artificial sweetener equivalent to
*   1/4 cup sugar*

3/4 cup lime juice
1/2 cup orange-flavored liqueur
1 cup white tequila
Ice

Purée the strawberries, raspberries, blackberries and blueberries in a blender. Strain through a wire mesh strainer into a bowl and discard the seeds. Stir in the artificial sweetener, lime juice, orange liqueur and tequila. Return to the blender and add ice. Blend to frozen drink consistency or serve the margaritas over ice in glasses. You may use sugar instead of artificial sweetener but it won't be as "skinny."

Chocolate Martinis

Serves 8

Chocolate syrup
1 1/2 ounces caramel-flavored vodka
1 ounce milk chocolate-flavored liqueur
1 ounce white chocolate-flavored liqueur
1 ounce hazelnut-flavored liqueur
1 ounce half-and-half
Ice

Add chocolate syrup to martini glasses and swirl to coat. Combine the vodka, milk chocolate liqueur, white chocolate liqueur, hazelnut liqueur and half-and-half in a cocktail shaker. Add ice. Cover and shake to mix well. Strain into the prepared glasses.

Valentine Mimosa

Serves 1

1 ounce Noble™ 100% pure blood orange juice
3 ounces Prosecco or Champagne

Pour the blood orange juice into a fluted glass and top with the Prosecco.

Mojitos

Serves 6 to 8

Juice of 7 limes   *3 cups club soda*
30 mint leaves   *1 cup white rum*
1 cup simple syrup

Combine the lime juice and mint in a pitcher and crush the mint with a muddler or pestle. Stir in the simple syrup, club soda and rum.

How to Make Simple Syrup

So many of our favorite summer cocktails start off with a basic simple syrup recipe. Combine two cups sugar and one cup water in a small saucepan and cook over medium heat for three to five minutes or until the sugar has completely dissolved, stirring frequently. Remove from the heat and let the mixture cool before using it in your favorite beverage. Substitute one and one-half teaspoons of simple syrup for every teaspoon of sugar you would normally use. Store the syrup in the refrigerator for up to two weeks.

LEMON RISOTTO FRITTERS WITH LEMON-CILANTRO DIPPING SAUCE

Makes 18 fritters

4 1/2 to 5 cups chicken broth
2 tablespoons butter
1 tablespoon olive oil
1 small onion, finely chopped
1 1/2 cups arborio rice
1/2 cup white wine
1 tablespoon lemon juice
1 teaspoon grated lemon zest
1/2 teaspoon sea salt
1/4 teaspoon pepper

2 tablespoons butter
2 eggs
1 cup all-purpose flour
1 cup dry bread crumbs
Vegetable oil for deep-frying
1/2 cup mayonnaise
1 1/2 teaspoons minced fresh cilantro
1 garlic clove, minced
1 teaspoon grated lemon zest
1 teaspoon lemon juice

For the fritters: Heat the broth in a saucepan and keep warm. Heat 2 tablespoons butter and the olive oil in a large skillet. Add the onion and sauté for 2 to 3 minutes or until tender. Add the rice and cook for 2 to 3 minutes, stirring constantly. Reduce the heat and stir in the wine and lemon juice. Cook until all of the liquid is absorbed, stirring constantly. Stir in the warm broth, 1/2 cup at a time. Cook until the liquid is absorbed, stirring constantly, before adding more broth. Cook until the risotto is creamy and the rice is almost tender. Stir in the lemon zest, salt, pepper and 2 tablespoons butter and cook until heated through. Spread in a 10×15-inch baking pan and let cool to room temperature. Chill, covered, for 1 hour.

Beat the eggs in a shallow bowl. Place the flour and bread crumbs in separate shallow bowls. Shape the risotto into 1 1/2-inch balls. Coat the fritters in the flour, then egg, then bread crumbs. Heat vegetable oil to 375 degrees in a deep fryer or electric skillet. Fry the fritters, a few at a time, until golden brown. Remove to paper towels to drain. Serve warm with Lemon-Cilantro Dipping Sauce.

For the dipping sauce: Combine the mayonnaise, cilantro, garlic, lemon zest and lemon juice in a bowl and mix well. Serve with the warm fritters.

SEARED TUNA

Serves 2 to 4

1 (1-inch-thick) fresh tuna loin
Coarsely ground pepper
3 tablespoons extra-virgin olive oil

Coat the tuna generously with pepper on all sides. Heat the olive oil in a skillet over high heat until very hot. Add the tuna and sear for 10 to 20 seconds per side or to desired doneness. Slice the tuna thinly and arrange on a serving plate. Serve with soy sauce and wasabi paste.

CRAB APPETIZERS

Makes 48 appetizers

1 jar Old English cheese spread,
  softened
6 tablespoons butter, softened
1 1/2 teaspoons mayonnaise
1/4 teaspoon garlic salt

1/4 teaspoon seasoned salt
1 (7-ounce) can crab meat, drained
6 English muffins, split
Paprika

Combine the cheese spread, butter, mayonnaise, garlic salt and seasoned salt in a bowl and mix well. Stir in the crab meat. Spread evenly over the muffin halves and sprinkle with paprika. Arrange on a baking sheet and freeze for 10 to15 minutes. Cut each muffin half into quarters and arrange on the baking sheet. Broil until bubbly.

Note: These can be made ahead and frozen in an airtight container until ready to broil.

Tangerine Shrimp Mojo

Serves 4 to 6

2 tablespoons olive oil
1 teaspoon chopped garlic
1/2 teaspoon ground cumin
1/2 teaspoon salt
1/4 teaspoon freshly ground pepper
1 1/2 pounds deveined peeled
    fresh shrimp

3 tablespoons rum
1/4 cup Noble™ 100% pure
    tangerine juice
1 tablespoon chopped fresh mint
1 tablespoon chopped fresh cilantro
Tangerine Salsa (below)

Heat the olive oil in a skillet. Add the garlic, cumin, salt, pepper and shrimp and sauté until the shrimp start to turn pink. Stir in the rum, tangerine juice, mint and cilantro. Sauté until the shrimp turn pink. Spoon the Tangerine Salsa onto serving plates and top with the shrimp.

Tangerine Salsa

1/4 cup finely chopped red onion
1/2 cup chopped fresh cilantro
1 cup chopped avocado
1 large tangerine, sectioned and chopped
1 small jalapeño chile, seeded and chopped
Salt and pepper to taste

Combine the onion, cilantro, avocado, tangerine, jalapeño chile, salt and pepper in a bowl and mix well.

Kasbah Wings

Serves 4 to 6

4 pounds chicken wings
Olive oil
4 1/2 teaspoons sea salt
1 tablespoon cinnamon
1 tablespoon ground cumin
1 teaspoon ground allspice

1 teaspoon cardamom
1 teaspoon garlic powder
1 teaspoon cayenne pepper
1 (9-ounce) jar mango chutney
2 tablespoons balsamic vinegar
Rum (optional)

Separate the wings at the joint and discard the tips. Remove the skin, if desired. Brush the wings lightly with olive oil. Mix the salt, cinnamon, cumin, allspice, cardamom, garlic powder and pepper together. Sprinkle over both sides of the wings. Place the wings in an airtight container and chill until ready to bake.

Pulse the chutney and vinegar in a food processor to finely chop the mango. Add a small amount of rum to thin, if desired.

Remove the wings from the refrigerator and pat dry with paper towels. Arrange the wings in a shallow baking pan coated with nonstick cooking spray. Bake at 450 degrees for 15 minutes. Reduce the heat to 375 degrees. Turn the wings over and bake for 10 minutes. Brush the wings with one-half of the sauce and bake for 10 minutes. Turn the wings over and brush with the remaining sauce. Bake for 10 to 15 minutes or until the chicken is cooked through. Let cool for 5 minutes before serving.

Avocado Deviled Eggs

Serves 24

12 hard-cooked eggs
2 small avocados
1/4 cup mayonnaise
1 teaspoon horseradish sauce

Juice of 1/2 lime
2 rosemary sprigs, finely chopped
Salt and pepper to taste
Emeril's® seasoning to taste

Slice the eggs in half and scoop out the yolks; set the whites aside. Mash the avocados and egg yolks together in a bowl. Add the mayonnaise, horseradish sauce, lime juice, rosemary, salt and pepper and mix well. Spoon evenly into the egg whites. Sprinkle with Emeril's seasoning.

Marmalade Meatballs

Serves 10

1 package frozen original-flavor
   mini meatballs
1 (16-ounce) jar orange marmalade
1/2 cup plum sauce (found in the
   Asian food aisle)

2 teaspoons chili sauce
1/2 teaspoon grated orange zest
1/2 cup orange juice
1 teaspoon Worcestershire sauce

Bake the meatballs according to package directions. Mix the marmalade, plum sauce, chili sauce, orange zest, orange juice and Worcestershire sauce in a 6-quart saucepan. Simmer for 10 minutes. Add the meatballs and simmer for 20 minutes, stirring occasionally. Remove to a chafing dish or slow cooker to keep warm for serving.

Bonfire Cheeseball

Serves 8

8 ounces cream cheese, softened
1 cup (4 ounces) shredded Cheddar cheese
2 to 3 tablespoons chopped cilantro
1 garlic clove, minced
1/2 teaspoon chili powder
1 teaspoon lime juice
1 teaspoon Worcestershire sauce
2 jalapeño chiles, seeded and chopped
8 slices bacon, crisp-cooked and crumbled
Salt and pepper to taste
1/2 cup chopped pecans, toasted

Combine the cream cheese, Cheddar cheese, cilantro, garlic, chili powder, lime juice, Worcestershire sauce, one-half of the jalapeño chiles and one-half of the bacon in a bowl and mix well. Season with salt and pepper. Shape into a ball. Mix the pecans, remaining jalapeño chiles and remaining bacon on a small plate. Roll the cheeseball in the pecan mixture to coat. Wrap in plastic wrap and chill for 1 hour to overnight. Unwrap and place on a serving plate. Serve with blue tortilla chips or crackers.

BLT Dip

Serves 8

1/2 cup mayonnaise
1/2 cup sour cream
1 1/2 cups bacon bits
1 bunch green onions, chopped
1 tomato, chopped

Combine the mayonnaise, sour cream, bacon bits, green onions and tomato in a bowl and mix well. Chill until ready to serve. Serve with crackers.

Sun-Dried Tomato Tapenade

Serves 8

1 (8-ounce) jar olive oil-packed sun-dried tomatoes
6 garlic cloves, coarsely chopped
9 kalamata olives, pitted
6 ounces goat cheese
1 loaf sourdough French bread, thinly sliced and toasted

Pulse the tomatoes, garlic and olives in a food processor until smooth. Remove to a decorative bowl and add a small serving spoon. Arrange on a platter with the cheese and bread. Encourage guests to spread goat cheese over the bread, top with the tapenade and enjoy.

Wine Pairing

Sauvignon blanc is the perfect wine to pair with this appetizer. The acidity of the wine can easily handle the acids of the sun-dried tomatoes and the tangy goat cheese.

Olive Tapenade

Serves 16

1 cup pitted assorted olives, such as
    green, kalamata, etc.
3 garlic cloves, minced
1/4 cup oil-packed sun-dried tomatoes,
    drained and chopped
1/4 cup pine nuts, lightly toasted and
    chopped

2 Roma tomatoes, finely chopped
2 basil leaves, finely chopped
1/8 teaspoon grated lemon zest
1/8 teaspoon fresh lemon juice
Sliced French bread
Olive oil

Pulse the olives and garlic in a food processor until finely chopped. Remove to a bowl and stir in the sun-dried tomatoes, pine nuts, Roma tomatoes, basil, lemon zest and lemon juice. Brush the bread lightly with olive oil and toast. Serve with the tapenade.

Grape Expectations

Randy Chamberlin, founder of Grape Expectations, has over twenty-five years experience in the wine industry. He has a profound knowledge of wine derived from his time spent in wholesale distribution, attending countless wine seminars and tastings, and extensive training, as well as time spent as a sales representative and in management.

As his passion for wines grew, so did his desire to do something more, something special. And so, in early fall of 2008, Grape Expectations opened its doors, offering fine wines by the glass or by the bottle, wine flights, daily wine downs, and much more.

Not only is Grape Expectations a great place for light foods and good wine but also a place to discover and share thoughts and information about wine.

Fiesta Spinach Dip

Serves 8 to 10

1 jar medium salsa
1 (10-ounce) package frozen chopped
    spinach, thawed and drained
2 cups (8 ounces) Mexican-style
    shredded cheese
8 ounces cream cheese, cubed and
    softened

1 can pitted black olives, drained
    and chopped
2 tablespoons red wine vinegar
1 cup evaporated milk
Salt and pepper to taste

Combine the salsa, spinach, Mexican-style cheese, cream cheese, olives, vinegar, milk, salt and pepper in a bowl and mix well. Spoon into an 8×8-inch baking dish. Bake at 400 degrees for 12 to 15 minutes or until bubbly. Serve with crackers or baguette slices.

Onion Dip

Serves 12

12 to 16 ounces chopped onions (about 2 cups)
24 ounces cream cheese, softened
2 cups (8 ounces) grated Parmesan cheese
1/2 cup mayonnaise

Combine the onions, cream cheese, Parmesan cheese and mayonnaise in a bowl and mix well. Spoon into a baking dish. Bake at 425 degrees for 15 minutes or until the top is golden brown.

FIELD PEA SALSA

Serves 8 to 10

2 cans field peas with snaps, rinsed
    and drained
1 bunch green onions, chopped
2 cans whole kernel corn, drained
1 can tomatoes with green chiles,
    drained

1 large tomato, chopped
2 teaspoons minced garlic
1 bunch cilantro, stemmed
    and chopped
1 (16-ounce) bottle Italian
    salad dressing

Combine the peas, green onions, corn, tomatoes with green chiles, tomato, garlic, cilantro and salad dressing in a bowl and mix well. Chill for at least 4 hours, stirring occasionally. Drain the salsa and remove to a serving bowl. Serve with chips or as a side dish with grilled meats.

STRAWBERRY AND AVOCADO SALSA

Serves 10

2 cups chopped avocados
1 cup chopped strawberries
2 tablespoons chopped fresh cilantro

1 teaspoon minced seeded
    jalapeño chile
Juice of 1 lime
3/8 teaspoon salt

Combine the avocados, strawberries, cilantro, jalapeño chile, lime juice and salt in a bowl and mix gently. Serve with chips.

Careful Cutting

A cutting board that slides is a kitchen hazard. Keep yours secure by placing a dish towel underneath it. This will keep your cutting board in one place for easy and safe chopping.

BREAKFAST & BRUNCH

BOATER'S PARADISE

Winter Haven has been, and always will be, known as the Chain of Lakes City. With over fifty lakes within its boundaries and two chains connecting nine and sixteen lakes, Winter Haven truly is a boater's paradise. Though linking the lakes began almost one hundred years ago as a way to conveniently maneuver through the town on water, the boom of the roaring '20s sped up the connection of additional lakes via the first engineered canals as Florida was flooded with sunshine seekers and vacation dollars. The most serious construction got under way during the Depression thanks to the WPA dollars and the Civilian Conservation Corps, which created the now 6,000-acre Chain of Lakes.

Winter Haven was known in its first heyday as a playground to celebrities such as Elvis Presley, Frank Sinatra, and Esther Williams, who visited the area and played in Florida's first theme Park, Cypress Gardens. Today, the Chain is in a period of resurgence as it hosts world class water skiers, fishing tournaments, wildlife, Legoland's newest theme park, and even a church service, not to mention the week-long Chain of Lakes Festival featuring boat races, sunset celebrations, and boat parades.

Orange-Pecan French Toast

Serves 6 to 8

1 cup packed brown sugar
1/3 cup butter, melted
2 tablespoons light corn syrup
2/3 cup chopped pecans
12 (3/4-inch-thick) slices French bread
2 eggs
3 egg whites
2 teaspoons grated orange zest
1 cup orange juice
1/2 cup milk
3 tablespoons granulated sugar
1 1/2 teaspoons cinnamon
1 teaspoon vanilla extract
1 tablespoon confectioners' sugar

Combine the brown sugar, melted butter and corn syrup in a bowl and mix well. Pour evenly into a greased 9×13-inch baking dish and sprinkle with the pecans. Fit the bread slices in a single layer over the pecans. Whisk the eggs, egg whites, orange zest, orange juice, milk, granulated sugar, cinnamon and vanilla in a bowl. Pour evenly over the bread, pressing with the back of a spoon to ensure the bread absorbs liquid. Chill, covered for 1 hour to overnight.

Remove from the refrigerator and let stand for 20 minutes. Bake, uncovered, at 350 degrees for 35 minutes or until golden brown. Dust with the confectioners' sugar and serve.

CRISPY BLUEBERRY BREAKFAST CASSEROLE

Serves 8

6 glazed doughnuts
1/2 cup blueberries
6 eggs
3/4 cup half-and-half
1/4 cup water
1/4 cup (1/2 stick) butter, cut into small pieces
2 packages brown sugar and cinnamon
*   instant oatmeal mix*

Cut each doughnut into 8 pieces and layer in a greased baking dish. Sprinkle with the blueberries. Whisk the eggs, half-and-half and water in a bowl and pour evenly over the doughnut pieces. Dot with the butter and sprinkle with the oatmeal mix. Bake at 350 degrees for 35 minutes.

Before You Start

Gather all of your ingredients in bowls prior to starting the recipe.

HAM AND ORANGE-HORSERADISH BISCUITS

Serves 12

1 1/4 cups baking mix
1/2 cup (2 ounces) shredded Gruyère cheese
1/2 cup water
Orange-Horseradish Spread (below)
12 slices ham

Mix the baking mix and cheese in a bowl. Add the water and stir just until mixed. Drop the dough by tablespoonfuls onto a greased baking sheet. Bake at 400 degrees for 10 minutes or until firm and lightly browned. Remove to a wire rack to cool. Slice each biscuit in half and spread with Orange-Horseradish Spread. Place one slice of ham between biscuit halves and serve.

ORANGE-HORSERADISH SPREAD

1/2 cup sour cream
1 tablespoon orange marmalade
1 tablespoon whole grain mustard
1 tablespoon prepared horseradish
1/4 teaspoon pepper

Combine the sour cream, orange marmalade, mustard, horseradish and pepper in a bowl and mix well. Chill until ready to use.

Shredding Semi-Soft Cheese

Make shredding semi-soft cheese easier by freezing the cheese for about 30 minutes or until firm before shredding.

So-Fine Shrimp and Cheddar Grits

Serves 6

1 cup chopped bacon
2 cups thinly sliced sweet mini
peppers
1/2 cup thinly sliced onion
2 jalapeño chiles, seeded and
thinly sliced
1 1/2 pounds deveined peeled fresh
medium shrimp
Hot red pepper sauce to taste
Cheddar Grits (below)
Chopped green onions for garnish
Shredded Cheddar cheese for garnish

Cook the bacon in a skillet until crisp. Remove and discard all but 1 tablespoon of the bacon drippings from the skillet. Add the sweet peppers, onion and jalapeño chiles to the skillet and sauté until tender. Add the shrimp and sauté until the shrimp turn pink. Season with hot sauce. Serve over warm Cheddar Grits and garnish with green onions and cheese.

Cheddar Grits

1 1/2 cups chicken broth
1 1/2 cups milk
3/4 cup quick-cooking grits
1/4 teaspoon salt
1 cup (4 ounces) shredded Cheddar cheese

Bring the broth and milk to a boil in a saucepan. Stir in the grits and salt. Bring to a boil and reduce the heat. Cook for 5 minutes or until thickened, stirring occasionally. Stir in the cheese.

SHRIMP QUICHE

Serves 16

2 frozen unbaked pie shells
5 eggs
1 1/2 cups milk
1/4 teaspoon salt
1/8 teaspoon pepper
1/8 teaspoon dry mustard
2 teaspoons Worcestershire sauce
1 1/2 cups (6 ounces) grated
   Parmesan cheese
1 cup (4 ounces) shredded
   Swiss cheese

3 tablespoons all-purpose flour
8 ounces deveined peeled fresh
   shrimp, coarsely chopped
1 large red bell pepper,
   finely chopped
1 (10-ounce) package frozen
   chopped spinach, thawed and
   drained well
2 large avocados, sliced,
   for garnish
Chopped cilantro for garnish

Line the pie shells with heavy-duty foil. Bake at 400 degrees for 5 minutes. Remove the foil and bake for 5 minutes longer. Remove to a wire rack to cool.

Whisk the eggs, milk, salt, pepper, mustard and Worcestershire sauce in a large bowl. Combine the Parmesan cheese, Swiss cheese and flour in a bowl and toss to mix. Add to the eggs and mix well. Stir in the shrimp, bell pepper and spinach. Pour into the baked pie shells. Bake at 350 degrees for 50 to 55 minutes or until a knife inserted in the center comes out clean. Let stand for 5 minutes before serving. Garnish with avocado and cilantro.

SAVORY BREAKFAST STRATA

Serves 10

1 large red bell pepper, chopped
1 large Yukon Gold potato, peeled
   and chopped
1/2 cup chopped onion
2 tablespoons olive oil
8 eggs
3 cups milk
2 tablespoons Dijon mustard
1 teaspoon Worcestershire sauce
1 teaspoon seasoned salt

1 teaspoon pepper
1 (8-ounce) round Brie cheese
1 loaf sourdough bread,
   cubed
1 1/2 cups (6 ounces) shredded
   Swiss cheese
1/2 cup (2 ounces) grated
   Parmesan cheese
2 cups chopped ham

Sauté the bell pepper, potato and onion in the olive oil in a skillet for 10 to 12 minutes or until the vegetables are tender. Whisk the eggs, milk, Dijon mustard, Worcestershire sauce, salt and pepper in a bowl. Remove and discard the rind from the Brie cheese and cut into 1/2-inch cubes.

Layer the bread, vegetable mixture, Brie cheese, Swiss cheese, Parmesan cheese, ham and beaten eggs one-half at a time in a greased 9×13-inch baking dish. Chill, covered, overnight. Bake, uncovered, at 350 degrees for 50 to 60 minutes or until the center is set. Serve warm.

POTATO FRITTATA

Serves 8

2 tablespoons olive oil
1/2 cup chopped onion
16 ounces frozen hash brown potatoes, thawed
1 garlic clove, minced
1/2 teaspoon salt
1/4 teaspoon pepper
6 eggs
1/4 cup milk
1/4 cup (1 ounce) shredded Italian-blend cheese
4 slices bacon, crisp-cooked and crumbled
2 tablespoons chopped fresh basil

Heat the olive oil in an ovenproof skillet over medium heat. Add the onion and sauté for 4 minutes. Add the potatoes, garlic, salt and pepper and sauté over medium-low heat for 15 minutes or until the potatoes are tender. Whisk the eggs, milk, cheese, bacon and basil in a bowl and pour into the skillet. Cook, covered, for 2 minutes or until the eggs are almost set. Uncover and place under a preheated broiler for 4 minutes or until the top is golden brown. Cut into wedges and serve.

Sharp Knives

Make sure your knives are sharp. It will not only decrease your prep and presentation time but a sharp knife is also a safe knife.

LEMON-POPPY SEED SWEET BREAD

Serves 8 to 10

1 package pound cake mix
1 (3-ounce) package lemon gelatin
4 eggs
1/2 cup vegetable oil
3/4 cup apricot nectar

1 tablespoon lemon extract
1 tablespoon butter flavoring
2 tablespoons poppy seeds
1 1/2 cups confectioners' sugar
Juice of 1 large lemon

Mix the cake mix and gelatin together. Beat the eggs in a bowl. Beat in the oil, apricot nectar, lemon extract and butter flavoring. Stir in the dry ingredients. Stir in the poppy seeds. Pour into a greased and floured loaf pan. Bake at 325 degrees for 35 to 40 minutes. Remove to a wire rack and let cool for 10 minutes. Poke holes over the top of the bread with a fork. Mix the confectioners' sugar and lemon juice in a bowl and spread over the top of the warm bread.

BANANA BREAD

Serves 24

4 cups all-purpose flour
2 teaspoons baking soda
1/2 teaspoon salt
1 cup (2 sticks) butter, softened

2 cups sugar
4 eggs
6 large overripe bananas, mashed

Mix the flour, baking soda and salt together. Beat the butter and sugar in a mixing bowl until light and fluffy. Add the eggs, one at a time, beating well after each addition. Beat in the bananas. Stir in the dry ingredients. Pour into a greased and floured 9×13-inch baking pan. Bake at 350 degrees for 50 minutes or until the bread tests done.

Orange Spice Coffee Cake

Serves 8

6 tablespoons unsalted butter, softened

3/4 cup sugar

2 eggs

1 teaspoon vanilla extract

Grated zest of 1 large orange

2/3 cup sour cream

1 1/4 cups all-purpose flour

1 teaspoon baking powder

1/2 teaspoon baking soda

1/2 teaspoon salt

1 1/4 teaspoons cinnamon

Streusel (below)

Beat the butter and sugar in a mixing bowl until light and fluffy. Add the eggs, one at a time, beating well after each addition. Beat in the vanilla and orange zest. Add the sour cream and beat until smooth. Sift the flour, baking powder, baking soda, salt and cinnamon together. Beat into the batter gradually at low speed and beat until smooth. Pour into a greased and floured 9-inch round baking dish. Drop the Streusel by spoonfuls over the batter. Bake at 350 degrees for 45 minutes or until a wooden pick inserted in the center comes out clean. Remove to a wire rack to cool.

Streusel

1/4 cup granulated sugar

1/2 cup packed light brown sugar

1 1/2 teaspoons cinnamon

1/2 cup (1 stick) unsalted butter, melted

1 1/2 cups all-purpose flour

Mix the granulated sugar, brown sugar and cinnamon in a bowl. Add the melted butter and flour and stir until crumbly.

Wine Pairing

This dish pairs well with sparkling wine. A not overly sweet cake, it makes an excellent pairing with a slightly sweet sparkling wine or a demi-sec Champagne.

Pumpkin Bread

Makes 3 loaves

3 1/2 cups all-purpose flour
2 teaspoon baking soda
1 1/2 teaspoons salt
1 1/2 teaspoons cinnamon
1 teaspoon nutmeg
3 cups sugar

4 eggs, beaten
1 cup vegetable oil
2 cups canned pumpkin
2/3 cup water
3/4 cup raisins or golden raisins

Mix the flour, baking soda, salt, cinnamon, nutmeg and sugar in a bowl. Add the eggs, oil, pumpkin, water and raisins and mix well. Fill three nonstick standard loaf pans or seven nonstick 3×5-inch mini loaf pans half full. Bake at 350 degrees for 40 to 45 minutes or until a wooden pick inserted in the center comes out clean.

Blueberry Breakfast Cobbler

Serves 10

1/2 cup (1 stick) butter
1 cup all-purpose flour
1 cup sugar
2 teaspoons baking powder

3/4 cup milk
2 cups fresh blueberries
1/2 cup sugar
1/2 cup water

Melt the butter in a 9×13-inch baking pan in the oven. Tilt the pan to coat the bottom evenly with melted butter. Mix the flour, 1 cup sugar, baking powder and milk in a bowl. Pour evenly over the melted butter; do not stir. Sprinkle the blueberries over the batter and sprinkle 1/2 cup sugar over the blueberries. Pour the water evenly over the top; do not stir. Bake at 350 degrees for 50 minutes.

CHOCOLATE CHIP SCONES

Serves 8 to 10

3 1/4 cups all-purpose flour
1/2 cup plus 1 teaspoon sugar
1 tablespoon baking powder
1/4 teaspoon salt
2 cups dark chocolate chips
2 cups chilled whipping cream
1/4 teaspoon vanilla extract
2 tablespoons butter, melted
Additional sugar

Lightly grease two baking sheets. Mix the flour, sugar, baking powder and salt in a bowl. Stir in the chocolate chips. Add the cream and vanilla and stir just until mixed. Knead gently on a lightly floured surface for 1 to 2 minutes or until a soft dough forms. Divide the dough into three balls and pat each ball into a circle. Cut each circle into wedges. Place the wedges on the prepared baking sheets. Brush with melted butter and sprinkle with sugar. Bake at 375 degrees for 15 to 20 minutes or until lightly browned. Serve warm.

Chocolate Chips

Dust chocolate chips in a very small amount of flour before adding to batter; this will prevent the chips from sinking during baking.

BLUEBERRY MUFFINS

Makes 24 muffins

3 1/2 cups all-purpose flour
2/3 cup sugar
1 1/2 teaspoons salt
4 teaspoons baking powder
4 eggs

1/2 cup (1 stick) butter, melted
1 1/2 cups milk
2 cups blueberries
Topping (below)

Mix the flour, sugar, salt and baking powder in a large bowl. Combine the eggs, melted butter and milk in a bowl and mix well. Add to the dry ingredients and stir just until mixed. Fold in the blueberries. Fill paper-lined muffin cups two-thirds full. Spoon the Topping over the muffins. Bake at 400 degrees for 20 minutes or until a wooden pick inserted in the center comes out clean.

TOPPING

1 cup sugar
3/4 cup all-purpose flour
1/4 cup (1/2 stick) butter

Mix the sugar and flour in a bowl. Cut in the butter until crumbly.

SOUTHERN AMBROSIA

Serves 8

6 large Florida oranges, peeled and sectioned
1 (16-ounce) jar maraschino cherries, drained
1/2 cup shredded coconut (or to taste)
3/4 cup sugar (or to taste)

Combine the oranges, cherries, coconut and sugar in a bowl and mix well. Chill, covered, overnight. Serve cold.

CHAMPAGNE BERRIES

Serves 8

1 cup Champagne
1/4 cup sugar
1 teaspoon orange juice
1 pound fresh strawberries, sliced
6 ounces fresh blueberries

6 ounces fresh raspberries
1/2 cup heavy whipping cream
1 tablespoon sugar
8 amaretti cookies, crumbled

Combine the Champagne, 1/4 cup sugar, orange juice, strawberries, blueberries and raspberries in a bowl and toss gently. Chill, covered, for 30 minutes. Beat the cream in a bowl until soft peaks form. Beat in 1 tablespoon sugar. Top with the berries and cookies.

BROILED GRAPEFRUIT

Serves 2

1 grapefruit, at room temperature
3 tablespoons butter
1 teaspoon sugar
1/4 cup cinnamon-sugar (one part cinnamon to four parts sugar)

Slice the grapefruit in half. Cut around the membrane in the center of the fruit with a small serrated knife and remove. Cut around each section of the fruit to loosen. Insert 1 1/2 tablespoons butter into the center of each half and sprinkle each with 1/2 teaspoon sugar. Sprinkle 2 tablespoons cinnamon-sugar over each half. Arrange the grapefruit halves in a shallow baking pan. Broil until the top is browned and bubbling hot. Serve immediately.

This recipe was contributed by the Chalet Suzanne Restaurant & Inn.

Selecting Fruit

To choose the best fruit at the grocery store, give the fruit a firm squeeze. It should give slightly but not be too soft. Pick heavier fruit—it usually indicates more juice. Avoid fruit with soft spots. The fresher the fruit, the sweeter and more fragrant it will be.

Salads

Cypress Gardens—
America's Tropical Wonderland

Richard D. "Dick" Pope and his wife, Julie, opened Cypress Gardens in Winter Haven, Florida, on January 2, 1936. In its earliest days, Cypress Gardens consisted of a series of rustic paths winding through a stand of cypress trees interlaced with hand-dug canals and lined with azaleas and other plants the Popes gleaned from their neighbors. Electric boats guided guests through the canals to view the botanical gardens.

Over the years, Cypress Gardens also became known for its Southern belles and water ski shows. Many called it the "Water Ski Capital of the World" as it was the site of many of the sport's landmark firsts, and over fifty world records were broken there.

Today, the historic botanical gardens are now owned by the citizens of Polk County and leased to Legoland Florida, the world's largest Legoland theme park. Visitors can enjoy more than fifty rides, shows, attractions, restaurants, shopping, the Legoland Water Park, and the botanical gardens all found within the 150-acre interactive family theme park.

LEMON-SWEET CUCUMBER SALAD

Serves 6

1/2 cup sugar
1/2 teaspoon salt
1/2 teaspoon dried dill weed
1/2 teaspoon grated lemon zest
1 tablespoon lemon juice
1/2 cup vinegar
2 large cucumbers
1/2 red onion, thinly sliced

Whisk the sugar, salt, dill weed, lemon zest, lemon juice and vinegar in a bowl. Cut the cucumbers into 1/4-inch slices and cut the slices in half. Add the cucumbers and onion to the bowl and mix well. Chill, covered, for 4 hours to overnight.

Sweet Magnolia's Tea Bistro

This recipe was contributed by Sweet Magnolia's Tea Bistro, which is located in the heart of historic downtown Auburndale. They offer an assortment of gourmet teas and coffees as well as fine meals and excellent desserts. The beautiful structure and the grounds hold significant historical value to the city and are recognized by the Auburndale Community Redevelopment Agency and Auburndale Historical Preservation Committees.

Nutty Broccoli Salad

Serves 12

1 cup (or more) mayonnaise
1/2 cup sugar
2 tablespoons vinegar
1 tablespoon grated onion
2 bunches broccoli, cut into small florets
1 to 2 cups chopped fresh vegetables, such as
*   radishes, carrots, celery or cauliflower*
8 slices bacon, crisp-cooked and crumbled
1/2 cup raisins
1/2 cup nuts

Whisk the mayonnaise, sugar, vinegar and onion in a bowl. Chill until ready to serve. Combine the broccoli, chopped vegetables, bacon, raisins and nuts in a bowl and toss to mix. Add the dressing and toss to coat. Stir in additional mayonnaise, if needed. The specific vegetables are not as important in this salad, but it is prettier with some color. The quantity of vegetables is also not critical.

Variations

You may substitute sweetened dried cranberries for the raisins. Cashews, slivered almonds, and sunflower kernels work well in this salad. For autumn flavors, use sweetened dried cranberries and dried pumpkin seeds.

Chick-Pea Salad

Serves 4

2 tablespoons fresh lemon juice
4 teaspoons extra-virgin olive oil
1/2 teaspoon honey
1 garlic clove, pressed
1 (15-ounce) can chick-peas, rinsed and drained
8 to 10 grape tomatoes, halved
1/3 cup finely chopped strawberry onion
2 tablespoons chopped fresh basil
2 tablespoons chopped fresh flat-leaf parsley
1/3 cup freshly grated Parmesan cheese
Kosher salt to taste
Freshly ground pepper to taste

Whisk the lemon juice, olive oil, honey and garlic in a bowl. Add the chick-peas, tomatoes, onion, basil, parsley and cheese and toss gently to mix. Season with salt and pepper. Chill until ready to serve. Serve chilled or at room temperature.

BEST POTATO SALAD

Serves 6

Salt to taste
2 pounds Yukon Gold potatoes
1 egg
1/2 bunch green onions, sliced
1 cup mayonnaise
1/4 cup Dijon mustard
1/4 cup dill pickle relish, with juice

Juice of 1/2 lemon
1/2 small red onion, minced
Pepper to taste
2 tablespoons chopped
  flat-leaf parsley
Extra-virgin olive oil for drizzling

Fill a pot with cold water and add a generous amount of salt. Add the unpeeled potatoes and egg. Bring to a simmer and cook for 12 minutes. Remove the egg and continue cooking the potatoes for 6 to 8 minutes longer or under tender. Drain and let cool.

Remove and reserve some of the green onions for garnish. Combine the remaining green onions, mayonnaise, Dijon mustard, pickle relish, lemon juice and red onion in a bowl and mix well. Season with salt and pepper. Peel the egg and grate into the bowl. Peel the cooled potatoes and break apart with clean hands. Add the potatoes to the bowl and toss to mix. Sprinkle with the parsley and reserved green onions. Drizzle with olive oil and serve.

WARM SWEET POTATO SALAD

Serves 6

3 tablespoons olive oil
Juice of 1 small lime
1 teaspoon ground cumin
1 teaspoon garlic powder
1 teaspoon paprika, or to taste
Salt and black pepper to taste

Red pepper flakes to taste (optional)
1 red onion, finely chopped
1 can black beans, drained
9 sweet potatoes, peeled and
   cut into cubes

Whisk the olive oil, lime juice, cumin, garlic powder, paprika, salt, black pepper and red pepper flakes in a large bowl. Stir in the onion and beans. Cook the sweet potatoes in a saucepan of boiling water until tender; drain. Add the warm sweet potatoes to the dressing and toss to mix. Serve warm or chilled.

PEAR AND SPINACH SALAD

Serves 4

3 tablespoons balsamic vinegar
1 tablespoon Dijon mustard
1 garlic clove, minced
1/2 cup olive oil
Salt and freshly ground pepper to taste

9 ounces fresh spinach
2 pears, cored and chopped
1/2 cup crumbled feta cheese
1/4 cup sweetened dried cranberries
1/4 cup sliced almonds

Whisk the vinegar, Dijon mustard and garlic in a bowl. Add the olive oil in a fine stream, whisking constantly until mixed well. Season with salt and pepper. Combine the spinach, pears, cheese, cranberries and almonds in a bowl and toss to mix. Add the dressing and toss to coat.

SPINACH SALAD

Serves 4

1/2 cup olive oil
1/4 cup white vinegar
3/4 cup sugar
1 tablespoon poppy seeds
1/4 teaspoon paprika
4 cups baby spinach, rinsed and dried
1 1/2 cups strawberries, sliced
1/3 cup sliced almonds

Combine the olive oil, vinegar, sugar, poppy seeds and paprika in a jar with a tight-fitting lid and seal tightly. Shake to mix. Chill until ready to use. Combine the spinach, strawberries and almonds in a bowl and toss to mix. Add the dressing and toss to coat.

Cutting Boards

Place a clean, thin rubber mat under bamboo and wooden cutting boards to eliminate movement when in use.

Sun-Dried Tomato Pasta Salad

Serves 8

*16 ounces fusilli, cooked with 1 teaspoon kosher salt,
  drained and cooled*
16 ounces fresh tomatoes, chopped
3/4 cup black olives, pitted and chopped
1 package crumbled feta cheese
8 oil-packed sun-dried tomato halves, drained and chopped
1 cucumber, chopped
Sun-Dried Tomato Dressing (below)
1 cup (4 ounces) freshly grated Parmesan cheese
3/4 cup chopped flat-leaf parsley

Combine the pasta, fresh tomatoes, olives, feta cheese, sun-dried tomatoes, cucumber and Sun-Dried Tomato Dressing in a bowl and toss to coat. Add the Parmesan cheese and parsley and toss to mix.

Sun-Dried Tomato Dressing

7 oil-packed sun-dried tomato halves, drained
3 tablespoons red wine vinegar
6 tablespoons olive oil
3 garlic cloves
1 teaspoon capers
1 teaspoon kosher salt
1 teaspoon freshly ground pepper

Process the tomatoes, vinegar, olive oil, garlic, capers, salt and pepper in a food processor until almost smooth.

GREEK PASTA SALAD

Serves 6 to 8

1/2 cup (or more) olive oil
1/2 cup red wine vinegar
1 1/2 teaspoons garlic powder
1 1/2 teaspoons dried basil
1 1/2 teaspoons dried oregano
3/4 teaspoon pepper
3/4 teaspoon sugar
2 1/2 cups tri-color rotini,
   cooked and drained
2 cups cherry tomatoes, halved

1/2 cup chopped green onions
3/4 cup crumbled feta cheese
1 cup sliced green bell pepper,
   finely chopped
1 (4-ounce) can pitted black
   olives, finely chopped
1 (4-ounce) can pitted green
   olives, finely chopped
3/4 cup sliced pepperoni,
   cut in half

Whisk the olive oil, vinegar, garlic powder, basil, oregano, pepper and sugar in a large bowl. Add the pasta, tomatoes, green onions, cheese, bell pepper, black olives, green olives and pepperoni and toss to mix. Chill, covered, for 2 hours to overnight. Stir in additional olive oil, if needed.

Wine Pairing

French rosé wines are aromatic and dry. The acidity of the wine counters the acidity of the tomatoes, making it an excellent choice for pairing with this dish.

Rice Salad

Serves 6 to 8

1 (7-ounce) package long grain and wild rice mix
4 ounces feta cheese, crumbled
1/2 cup chopped yellow bell pepper
1/2 cup chopped green onions
1/2 cup chopped parsley
1 can baby artichoke hearts, drained and chopped
1 cup cherry tomatoes, halved
2/3 cup pine nuts, toasted
1/3 cup olive oil
2 tablespoons white wine vinegar
1/4 teaspoon dried tarragon
Salt and pepper to taste

Cook the rice according to package directions; let cool. Combine the rice, cheese, bell pepper, green onions, parsley, artichokes, tomatoes and pine nuts in a bowl and toss to mix. Whisk the olive oil, vinegar, tarragon, salt and pepper in a bowl. Add to the salad and toss to coat. Chill, covered, for at least 4 hours.

LAKESIDE CHICKEN SALAD

Serves 4

3 boneless skinless chicken breasts, cooked and cooled
1 avocado, mashed
2 tablespoons lime juice
2 tablespoons light mayonnaise
2 tablespoons finely chopped green onions
2 tablespoons chopped cilantro
Salt and pepper to taste
Lettuce leaves or croissant halves

Shred the chicken into a bowl. Scoop the avocado on top of the chicken and sprinkle with the lime juice. Add the mayonnaise and mix well. Stir in the green onions and cilantro and season with salt and pepper. Chill before serving. Serve over a bed of lettuce or spread between croissant halves.

Juicier Citrus

To extract the most juice, microwave citrus on High for about 10 seconds.

CRUNCHY ASIAN CHICKEN SALAD

Serves 6

1 package chicken-flavored ramen noodles
3 tablespoons butter
1/4 cup red wine vinegar
2 tablespoons sugar
1/2 cup vegetable oil
2 tablespoons water
2 cups cubed cooked chicken breast
3 green onions, chopped
1 pound shredded cabbage
1 can mandarin oranges, drained (optional)
3/4 cup slivered almonds, toasted
1 tablespoon sesame seeds, toasted

Remove the seasoning packet from the noodles and set aside. Crush the noodles. Melt the butter in a saucepan and add the crushed noodles. Sauté until the noodles are golden brown. Remove from the heat and let cool. Combine the vinegar, sugar, oil, water and contents of the seasoning packet in a jar with a tight-fitting lid and seal tightly. Shake to mix. Combine the chicken, green onions, cabbage, oranges, almonds and sesame seeds in a bowl and toss to mix. Add desired amount of dressing and toss to coat. Top with the noodles.

SIDE DISHES

BOK TOWER

When Bok Tower Gardens founder Edward W. Bok immigrated to America at age six, he did not understand the language, customs, or culture. Through determination and hard work, he became a highly successful publisher, Pulitzer Prize–winning author, respected humanitarian, and advocate of world peace and the environment. Bok's grandmother told him to "make the world a bit better or more beautiful because you have lived in it."

Discover why Bok Tower Gardens is "a spot of beauty second to none in the country." Through its historic landscape gardens, unique Singing Tower carillon, and magnificent 1930s Mediterranean-style mansion, the Gardens offer unparalleled opportunities for artistic, cultural, personal, and spiritual enrichment.

ORANGE-SCENTED ORZO WITH DRIED CHERRIES

Serves 4

6 cups water
1 cup orzo
1/4 teaspoon crumbled saffron threads
2 teaspoons grated orange zest
2 tablespoons orange juice
1 tablespoon Grand Marnier or other orange-flavored Cognac
Salt to taste
3 tablespoons olive oil
1/3 cup dried tart cherries
2 tablespoons toasted slivered almonds
1 green onion, sliced diagonally

Heat the water in a saucepan to boiling. Stir in the orzo and saffron. Cook for 8 minutes or until the pasta is tender. Drain and rinse with cold water; drain well. Whisk the orange zest, orange juice, Grand Marnier and salt in a bowl. Add the olive oil in a fine stream, whisking constantly until mixed well. Add the pasta and toss to coat. Stir in the cherries, almonds and green onion. Serve at room temperature.

SESAME NOODLES

Serves 6

16 ounces linguini
Salt to taste
1 1/2 teaspoons dark sesame oil
Grated zest and juice of 1 lime
3 tablespoons thinly sliced green onions
1/2 cup grated carrot
2 tablespoons tahini or creamy
    peanut butter
2 tablespoons dark sesame oil
4 1/2 teaspoons soy sauce
1/4 cup water

2 teaspoons minced garlic
2 teaspoons minced peeled
    fresh ginger
2 teaspoons rice vinegar
1 teaspoon sugar
1/2 teaspoon red pepper flakes
1 pinch of salt
3 tablespoons chopped fresh cilantro
1 tablespoon sesame seeds,
    lightly toasted

Cook the linguini in a saucepan of boiling salted water for 9 minutes or until tender. Drain and rinse with cold water; drain well. Combine the linguini, 1 1/2 teaspoons sesame oil, lime zest and lime juice in a large bowl and toss to coat. Add the green onions and carrot and toss to mix. Process the tahini, 2 tablespoons sesame oil, soy sauce, water, garlic, ginger, vinegar, sugar, red pepper flakes and pinch of salt in a blender until smooth. Pour over the pasta and sprinkle with the cilantro and sesame seeds. Serve with chicken, pork or sandwiches.

BUTTERNUT SQUASH RISOTTO

Serves 4

3 cups chicken broth
1 cup puréed cooked butternut squash
Salt and pepper to taste
1 teaspoon olive oil
2 garlic cloves, chopped
1/4 cup chopped shallots
2 ounces chopped pancetta
1 cup arborio rice
1/4 cup dry white wine
1/4 cup (1 ounce) freshly grated Parmesan cheese

Bring the broth and squash to a boil in a saucepan over medium-high heat. Reduce the heat to low and simmer. Season with salt and pepper. Heat the olive oil in a saucepan over medium heat. Add the garlic, shallots, pancetta and rice and sauté for 3 minutes. Add the wine and cook until the wine is absorbed, stirring constantly. Stir in the hot broth, 1 ladleful at a time. Cook until the liquid is absorbed, stirring constantly, before adding more broth. Cook until all of the broth is used and the risotto is creamy and tender. Stir in the cheese and remove from the heat.

Choosing a Wine

When the recipe calls for wine, make sure to use a wine you enjoy drinking. If you like to drink it, you will surely like it in the dish!

BAKED BROWN RICE

Serves 4 to 6

1 (10-ounce) can beef consommé
1 (10-ounce) can French onion soup
1/4 cup (1/2 stick) butter, melted
1 cup uncooked rice

Combine the consommé, onion soup, melted butter and rice in a bowl and mix well. Pour into a 9×13-inch baking dish. Bake, covered, at 350 degrees for 45 minutes.

COCONUT RICE

Serves 8

2 cups jasmine rice
1 tablespoon unsalted butter
1 (13-ounce) can unsweetened
   coconut milk

1 cup water
1/4 teaspoon sea salt or kosher salt
1 cinnamon stick

Rinse the rice in a wire mesh strainer under cold running water for 2 minutes; drain well. Melt the butter in a 3-quart saucepan over medium heat. Add the rice and sauté for 2 minutes. Stir in the coconut milk, water and salt and bring to a boil. Add the cinnamon stick and reduce the heat to low. Cook, covered, for 20 minutes. Remove from the heat and let stand for 5 minutes. Remove and discard the cinnamon stick. Fluff the rice with a fork. Serve hot with a spicy entrée such as Jamaican jerk chicken or pork kabobs and mango salsa.

Asparagus Tart

Serves 4

1 sheet frozen puff pastry, thawed
2 cups (8 ounces) shredded Gruyère cheese
1 1/2 pounds asparagus spears
1 tablespoon olive oil
Juice of 1 lemon
1/2 cup (2 ounces) grated Parmesan cheese
Salt and pepper to taste

Roll the pastry to a 10×16-inch rectangle on a floured surface and place on a nonstick baking sheet. Prick the surface of the pastry with a fork, leaving a 1-inch border. Fold in and pleat the border to form a rim. Bake at 400 degrees for 15 minutes or until golden brown.

Sprinkle the tart shell evenly with the Gruyère cheese. Fit the asparagus over the cheese, alternating ends and tips, trimming the ends if necessary to fit. Brush with the olive oil and sprinkle with the lemon juice. Sprinkle with the Parmesan cheese, salt and pepper. Bake at 400 degrees for 20 to 25 minutes or until the asparagus is tender.

Wine Pairing

A pinot blanc from Oregon, with its elegant fruit and mineral style, will pair very nicely with the unusual metallic flavor of the asparagus. Try to avoid oaky, buttery, or high-acidity wines.

PEPPER THREE-BEAN BAKE

Serves 8

4 pepper bacon slices, chopped
2 cups finely chopped onions
6 garlic cloves, minced
3/4 cup tomato sauce
1/3 cup packed brown sugar
1 tablespoon cider vinegar
1 tablespoon honey
1 tablespoon Dijon mustard

1 teaspoon smoked paprika
1/2 teaspoon kosher salt
1/2 teaspoon black pepper
1/4 teaspoon ground red pepper
1 (15-ounce) can each black beans,
  Great Northern beans and
  chick-peas, rinsed and drained

Heat a large nonstick skillet over medium-high heat. Sauté the bacon for 5 minutes or until crisp. Remove the bacon from the skillet with a slotted spoon, reserving 1 1/2 tablespoons drippings in the skillet. Sauté the onions and garlic in the drippings in the skillet for 6 minutes or until tender, stirring occasionally. Remove from the heat and let cool slightly.

Whisk the tomato sauce, brown sugar, vinegar, honey, Dijon mustard, paprika, salt, black pepper and red pepper together in a large bowl. Stir in the onion mixture, beans and chick-peas. Spoon into a 7x11-inch glass or ceramic baking dish coated with nonstick cooking spray. Crumble the bacon over the top. Bake, covered, at 325 degrees for 30 minutes. Uncover and bake for 30 minutes longer.

BROCCOLI AND CAULIFLOWER IN LEMON VINAIGRETTE

Serves 6

1 bunch broccoli, cut into florets
1 head cauliflower, cut into florets
3 tablespoons capers
Juice of 1 lemon
3 tablespoons extra-virgin olive oil
2 garlic cloves, crushed
1 small shallot, minced
Salt and pepper to taste

Steam the broccoli and cauliflower in a steamer for 5 minutes. Remove to a colander and rinse with cool water; drain well. Combine the broccoli, cauliflower and capers in a bowl and toss to mix. Whisk the lemon juice, olive oil, garlic, shallot, salt and pepper in a bowl. Add to the vegetables and toss to coat. Serve immediately.

CREAMY CORN CASSEROLE

Serves 10 to 12

1 can whole kernel yellow corn,
 partially drained
1 can cream-style corn
1 cup sour cream

2 eggs, beaten
1 package corn muffin mix
1/2 cup (1 stick) butter, melted

Combine the whole kernel corn, cream-style corn, sour cream, eggs, muffin mix and melted butter in a bowl and mix well. Pour into a lightly oiled baking pan. Bake at 350 degrees for 50 to 60 minutes.

GRUYÈRE-ROASTED POTATOES

Serves 8 to 10

3 pounds Yukon Gold potatoes, sliced
2 cups (8 ounces) shredded Gruyère
 cheese
Sea salt and pepper to taste

2 eggs
2 cups heavy whipping cream
2 garlic cloves, minced
1/4 teaspoon freshly grated nutmeg

Blanch the potatoes in a saucepan of boiling water for 2 minutes; drain. Layer the potatoes and cheese alternately in a 9×13-inch baking dish coated with nonstick cooking spray, seasoning each layer lightly with salt and pepper. Whisk the eggs, cream, garlic and nutmeg in a bowl. Pour evenly over the potatoes and cheese. Bake at 350 degrees for 1 hour. Serve hot.

MANGO-SERRANO RELISH

Serves 4

2 tablespoons fresh lime juice
1 tablespoon honey
2 tablespoons olive oil
2 mangoes, peeled, pitted and chopped
2 green onions, thinly sliced
1 serrano chile, thinly sliced
Sea salt and pepper to taste

Whisk the lime juice, honey and olive oil in a bowl. Add the mangoes, green onions, serrano chile, salt and pepper and mix well. Let stand for at least 15 minutes to allow the flavors to mingle. This can be made up to 24 hours ahead. Cover and chill. Allow to come to room temperature before serving.

Saving Time

Cleaning up as you cook saves time later.

Italian Peasant Soup

Serves 6 to 8

1 pound Italian sausage, casings
   removed and sausage chopped
2 onions, chopped
3 ribs celery, chopped
3 garlic cloves, chopped
2 (32-ounce) cans chicken broth
1 (14-ounce) can diced tomatoes

2 (14-ounce) cans cannellini
   beans, rinsed and drained
1 tablespoon dried oregano
1 tablespoon dried basil
6 cups fresh kale or spinach
Grated Parmesan cheese

Brown the sausage in a large saucepan over medium heat, stirring until crumbly; drain. Add the onions, celery and garlic and sauté until the vegetables are tender. Stir in the broth, tomatoes, beans, oregano and basil. Bring to a slow boil and cook, covered, for 10 minutes. Stir in the kale and cook until the kale is wilted. Sprinkle with the cheese and serve.

This recipe is from the personal collection of Ginny Johnston, Harry's Old Place.

Harry's Old Place

Harry's Old Place is, at its heart, a neighborhood restaurant. Folks drop by for a quick bite or to bring in friends while "doing the town." Located on the shore of Lake Ned in Winter Haven, Harry's Old Place offers a large assortment of fresh fish, great steaks, chicken, and pasta. The restaurant was first opened as Harriston's in 1980. A move to a larger location resulted in the name change when the restaurant returned to the original rustic building in Garden Grove in 1992.

Main Dishes

RITZ THEATRE

Built in 1925, the Ritz on Central Avenue in Winter Haven boasted an orchestra pit, a stage, dressing areas, and an organ. The theater was originally used for vaudeville shows and silent movies, followed by "talkies." In addition, some of Winter Haven's most prominent gentlemen cavorted across the stage dressed up as ladies in the "Mr. Winter Haven" pageants. Many generations of Central Florida residents fondly recall watching cartoons there on Saturday morning or stealing their first kiss in the balcony on Saturday night.

In the 1980s and 1990s, the Ritz reopened and closed several times until a group of citizens formed a nonprofit corporation, the Ritz Theatre 100, and purchased the building in 1997. Today, the Ritz Theatre's walls reverberate with joyful sounds of song and laughter, some tears, and even shouts of joy. The Ritz has once again become the grand social gathering place it once was.

Look for the Junior League of Greater Winter Haven's star on the Walk of Fame in the Lola Mann Lobby of the Ritz.

Source: http://www.ritzoncentral.com/history.html

Tequila Lime Shrimp with Roasted Chile Cream

Serves 4

1 cup vegetable oil
1/4 cup chopped garlic
1 bunch cilantro, coarsely chopped
1/4 cup lime juice
1/4 cup tequila

1 jalapeño chile, chopped
Salt and pepper to taste
20 large (14- to 16-count) fresh shrimp,
    peeled and deveined, shells reserved
Roasted Chile Cream (below)

Process the oil, garlic, cilantro, lime juice, tequila, jalapeño chile, salt and pepper in a blender until almost smooth. Pour over the shrimp in a bowl. Marinate in the refrigerator for at least 2 hours but no longer than 3 hours. Remove the shrimp and discard the marinade. Thread 5 shrimp onto each of 4 skewers and grill until the shrimp turn pink. Serve with the Roasted Chile Cream, Coconut Rice (page 75) and simmered black beans.

Roasted Chile Cream

4 large poblano chiles
1 tablespoon vegetable oil
3 garlic cloves, crushed
20 shrimp shells

1/4 cup tequila
4 cups heavy whipping cream
1 bunch cilantro
Sea salt and pepper to taste

Lay the poblano chiles on a gas burner grate. Roast until blackened, turning frequently with tongs. Remove to a bowl and cover. Let steam for 10 to 15 minutes. Peel the chiles, removing the stems and seeds. Purée the chiles in a food processor or blender.

Heat the oil in a saucepan over medium-high heat until almost smoking. Add the garlic and shrimp shells and sauté for 3 to 5 minutes. Add the tequila carefully as it may ignite. Cook until the tequila evaporates. Stir in the cream and cilantro and reduce the heat to medium. Simmer until the sauce is reduced by one-half, stirring occasionally. Stir in the puréed chiles, salt and pepper. Simmer gently until heated through. Strain through a wire mesh into a saucepan. Keep warm over very low heat.

BBQ Shrimp

Serves 4

1/4 cup finely chopped onion
1 tablespoon brown sugar
1 tablespoon dry mustard
1 teaspoon vinegar
1 teaspoon garlic powder
1/2 cup ketchup
2 tablespoons chopped fresh rosemary
Hot red pepper sauce to taste
24 extra-large peeled fresh shrimp
Wooden skewers

Combine the onion, brown sugar, mustard, vinegar, garlic powder, ketchup, rosemary and hot sauce in a shallow bowl and mix well. Thread 6 shrimp each onto 4 wooden skewers that have been soaked in cold water. Add the shrimp to the barbecue sauce and turn to coat. Marinate in the refrigerator for 1 hour. Remove the shrimp and discard the marinade. Grill the shrimp on a preheated grill until the shrimp turn pink. Serve with lime wedges.

Prevent Spinning Skewers

Turning skewers that are loaded with meats and vegetables can sometimes be a difficult task. To prevent spinning, thread the meat and vegetables onto two parallel skewers.

SHRIMP MANELLI

Serves 10 to 12

2 cups (4 sticks) butter
2 cups (4 sticks) margarine
4 lemons, cut in half
3/4 cup Worcestershire sauce
2 teaspoons garlic salt
1 tablespoon oregano
2 teaspoons basil
4 teaspoons rosemary

1/2 cup pepper
4 teaspoons salt
1 tablespoon Tony Chachere's
    Original Creole seasoning
1 teaspoon Tabasco sauce
5 pounds deveined peeled
    fresh shrimp

Melt the butter and margarine in a saucepan over medium heat. Stir in the lemons, Worcestershire sauce, garlic salt, oregano, basil, rosemary, pepper, salt, Creole seasoning and Tabasco sauce. Bring to a boil and reduce the heat. Simmer for 30 minutes. Spread the shrimp in shallow baking pans. Pour the sauce evenly over the shrimp. Broil the shrimp for 5 to 6 minutes or until the shrimp turn pink, turning once during cooking.

This recipe is from the personal collection of Ginny Johnston, Harry's Old Place.

Garlic Butter

Serve the Shrimp Manelli with crusty French bread brushed with garlic butter. To make garlic butter, mix one pound melted butter, one-half cup minced garlic, a dash of white pepper, a pinch of oregano, a pinch of tarragon, and three tablespoons granulated garlic.

SEASONED SHRIMP AND RICE

Serves 6

1 cup rice
2 cups water
Chopped fresh parsley
1 (10-ounce) can cream of shrimp soup
1 cup milk
1 1/2 teaspoons Chef Paul's seafood seasoning
Garlic powder to taste
4 teaspoons vegetable oil
1 small red bell pepper, chopped
1/2 cup chopped celery
2 teaspoons dried onion flakes
1 pound peeled cooked shrimp

Cook the rice and water in a saucepan over medium-low heat until the rice is tender and the liquid is absorbed, stirring frequently. Stir in parsley and keep warm. Mix the soup, milk, seafood seasoning and garlic powder in a bowl. Heat the oil in a skillet. Add the bell pepper and celery and sauté for 3 to 4 minutes. Stir in the onion flakes and soup mixture. Reduce the heat to low and simmer for 5 minutes. Stir in the shrimp and cook until heated through. Serve over the rice.

LUSCIOUS LOBSTER MAC AND CHEESE

Serves 8

1/4 cup (1/2 stick) butter
2 small shallots, finely chopped
2 garlic cloves, chopped
1 cup thinly sliced sweet mini peppers
5 tablespoons all-purpose flour
1/2 cup white wine
4 cups half-and-half
1/2 teaspoon paprika
1/4 teaspoon cayenne pepper
1/4 teaspoon freshly ground black
   pepper

1 bay leaf
2 cups (8 ounces) shredded sharp
   Cheddar cheese
2 cups (8 ounces) shredded Gruyère
   cheese
4 cups chopped cooked lobster meat
16 ounces pasta, cooked
   and drained
2 tablespoons butter
1 cup panko bread crumbs
1/4 cup chopped fresh parsley

Melt 1/4 cup butter in a large saucepan over medium heat. Add the shallots, garlic and sweet peppers and sauté until the vegetables are tender. Add the flour and cook for a few minutes, stirring constantly. Stir in the wine. Stir in the half-and-half gradually. Stir in the paprika, cayenne pepper, black pepper and bay leaf. Bring to a simmer and reduce the heat to low. Cook for 5 to 10 minutes or until the sauce is thickened and coats the back of a spoon, stirring frequently. Remove and discard the bay leaf.

Stir in the Cheddar cheese and Gruyère cheese gradually. Cook until the cheese is melted, stirring constantly. Stir in the lobster. Add the pasta and mix gently. Spoon into a greased large shallow baking dish.

Melt 2 tablespoons butter in a saucepan. Stir in the bread crumbs. Sprinkle the bread crumbs evenly over the mac and cheese and sprinkle with the parsley. Bake at 350 degrees for 30 minutes or until heated through and bubbly.

Maple-Glazed Salmon

Serves 4

4 salmon fillets, skinned and boned
1/3 cup maple syrup
3 tablespoons cider vinegar
1 tablespoon Dijon mustard
1 tablespoon soy sauce
1 tablespoon olive oil
2 garlic cloves, minced
1/4 teaspoon pepper

Place the fish in a sealable plastic bag. Whisk the maple syrup, vinegar, Dijon mustard, soy sauce, olive oil, garlic and pepper in a bowl and pour over the fish. Seal tightly and turn to coat. Marinate in the refrigerator for up to 8 hours. Remove the fish to a shallow baking pan lined with foil. Drizzle a small amount of the marinade over the fish and discard the remaining marinade. Cook under a preheated broiler for 10 to 15 minutes or until the fish begins to flake.

Variation

This recipe can also be prepared as an appetizer by using bite-sized portions of salmon served on cocktail picks. The cooking time may need to be reduced.

REALLY GOUDA ROASTED FISH

Serves 4

1 (1 1/2-pound) fillet of your favorite
   white fish
1 lemon
1/3 cup salsa

1/4 cup cashews, chopped
1/4 cup (1 ounce) shredded
   Gouda cheese

Arrange the fish in a shallow baking pan lined with foil. Grate the zest from the lemon and set aside. Squeeze the lemon and drizzle the juice over the fish. Top with the salsa, cashews and cheese. Roast at 400 degrees for 10 to 15 minutes or until the fish begins to flake. Garnish with the grated lemon zest and serve.

RUBY RED GRAPEFRUIT CHICKEN

Serves 4

6 chicken thighs or breasts
1/4 cup (1/2 stick) butter
2 ruby red grapefruit
1/2 cup whole cranberry sauce

1 tablespoon honey
1/4 teaspoon ground cloves
1/4 teaspoon salt
Hot cooked rice

Brown the chicken in the butter in a skillet. Remove the chicken to a shallow baking dish. Peel and section the grapefruit. Remove the membrane from the sections, catching any juice. Combine the juice, cranberry sauce, honey, cloves, and salt in a saucepan and mix well. Bring to a boil, stirring frequently. Stir in the grapefruit sections. Pour over the chicken and turn to coat. Bake at 350 degrees for 45 minutes, or until the chicken is cooked through, basting frequently with the sauce. Serve over hot cooked rice.

EASY CHICKEN POT PIE

Serves 6

2 frozen unbaked (9-inch) pie shells
2 cups cubed cooked chicken
12 ounces frozen peas and carrots
8 ounces frozen corn kernels
1 (10-ounce) can reduced-fat cream of potato soup
1 (10-ounce) can reduced-fat cream of chicken soup
Salt and pepper to taste

Thaw the pie shells for 15 minutes at room temperature. Combine the chicken, peas and carrots, corn, potato soup, chicken soup, salt and pepper in a bowl and mix well. Spoon into one of the pie shells.

Remove the remaining pie shell from the pan and roll out on a floured surface. Fit over the pie and crimp the edge with dampened fingers to seal. Cut vents in the top pastry. Place the pie in a shallow baking pan lined with foil. Bake at 375 degrees for 1 hour or until the crust is golden brown and the pie is bubbly.

Pie Crust

Cover the edge of the crust with foil if it is browning too quickly during baking.
Let stand for 10 minutes before serving.

Vitello Arabellas

Serves 4

4 (3-ounce) veal cutlets, lightly pounded
8 (16- to 20-count) deveined peeled fresh shrimp
8 large sea scallops
All-purpose flour for dusting
2 to 3 tablespoons olive oil
1/4 teaspoon saffron, crumbled
6 tablespoons dry white wine
1/2 cup heavy whipping cream
Sea salt and pepper to taste
16 ounces linguini, cooked and drained

Dust the veal, shrimp and scallops lightly with flour. Heat the olive oil and saffron in a large skillet until almost smoking. Add the shrimp and scallops in a single layer. Cook for 1 minute and turn. Add the veal and sear for 15 to 20 seconds per side. Stir in the wine and cream. Simmer for 2 minutes or until slightly thickened. Season with salt and pepper.

Divide the warm linguini among four serving plates. Top each with one veal cutlet, two shrimp and two scallops. Pour the sauce equally over the top. Serve with your favorite sautéed vegetables. Buon appetito!

This recipe was contributed by Arabellas Ristorante.

Tuscan-Style Porterhouse Steak

Serves 2

3 garlic cloves, finely chopped
1 tablespoon coarsely chopped thyme
5 fresh sage leaves
1 (1 1/2- to 2-inch-thick) Porterhouse steak
Salt and pepper to taste
Vegetable oil for brushing
1/2 cup extra-virgin olive oil

Spread the garlic, thyme and sage over the bottom of a deep dish or platter. Season the steak generously with salt and pepper. Brush vegetable oil over the grate on a preheated grill. Add the steak and grill to desired doneness.

Remove to the prepared platter and pour the olive oil over the steak. Turn the steak a few times to coat with the herbs and spoon the oil over the steak. Let stand for 3 to 5 minutes. Carve the steak and serve with the collected juices spooned over the meat.

Pan Searing Meat

When pan searing meat, resist the urge to turn it too soon. It is ready when it releases with ease; if it sticks, it is not ready to turn.

Citrus Flank Steak

Serves 4

1 1/4 pounds beef flank steak
1/2 cup Italian salad dressing
1/3 cup soy sauce
1/3 cup red wine
1 tablespoon grated orange zest
1/2 teaspoon dry mustard
1/8 teaspoon lemon pepper
1 garlic clove
1 rosemary sprig
3 lemon slices
3 tablespoons sliced green onions
Lemon or orange wedge for garnish

Place the steak in a sealable plastic bag. Whisk the salad dressing, soy sauce, wine, orange zest, mustard and lemon pepper in a bowl. Stir in the garlic, rosemary, lemon slices and green onions and pour over the steak. Seal tightly and turn to coat. Marinate in the refrigerator for 1 hour. Remove the steak and discard the marinade. Grill the steak on a preheated grill to desired doneness. Serve garnished with a lemon or orange wedge.

Backyard Florida Burgers

Serves 4

2 pounds ground chuck
1 teaspoon jerk seasoning
1/2 teaspoon garlic powder
1/2 teaspoon onion salt
1 teaspoon lemon pepper
1/2 teaspoon grated lime zest
1/2 teaspoon grated lemon zest

1/2 teaspoon grated orange zest
1 tablespoon fresh lime juice
1 tablespoon fresh lemon juice
1 tablespoon fresh orange juice
1 tablespoon hickory and brown sugar
 barbecue sauce

Combine the ground chuck, jerk seasoning, garlic powder, onion salt, lemon pepper, lime zest, lemon zest, orange zest, lime juice, lemon juice, orange juice and barbecue sauce in a bowl and mix well. Shape into 4 patties and chill for 30 minutes. Cook on a preheated grill to desired doneness.

Get the Most Juice Out of Your Citrus

When recipes call for fresh lime, lemon, or orange juice, roll the fruit on the counter using the palm of your hand before cutting in half. Don't be afraid to put a little muscle into it!

FIRE-ROASTED CHILI

Serves 4

1 1/4 pounds ground beef
1 small bell pepper, chopped into bite-size pieces
1 sweet onion, chopped into bite-size pieces
2 garlic cloves, minced
1 (16-ounce) can fire-roasted diced tomatoes
1 (10-ounce) can tomato soup
1 (16-ounce) can light red kidney beans
1 tablespoon chili powder
1 teaspoon ground cumin
1/2 teaspoon sea salt
1/2 teaspoon sugar

Brown the ground beef in a skillet, stirring until crumbly; drain. Sauté the bell pepper, onion and garlic in a nonstick saucepan over medium-high heat for 6 minutes or until tender. Stir in the ground beef, tomatoes, soup, kidney beans, chili powder, cumin, salt and sugar. Bring to a boil and reduce the heat. Simmer, covered, for 20 minutes. Serve in bowls or as a dip with tortilla chips.

Sautéing Vegetables

Adding a pinch of sea salt to vegetables during sauté will help them release their natural juices and caramelize.

Spicy Cajun Venison

Serves 4

1 venison backstrap	8 ounces cream cheese, softened
Dale's steak seasoning	3 tablespoons Cajun seasoning
2 jalapeño chiles, finely chopped	Bacon slices

Place the venison in a sealable plastic bag. Add the steak seasoning sparingly. Seal tightly and turn to coat. Marinate in the refrigerator for 2 hours.

Remove the meat to a work surface and discard the marinade. Cut a deep lengthwise slit in the venison and open to lay flat. Combine the jalapeño chiles, cream cheese and Cajun seasoning in a bowl and mix well. Spread over the venison and close the meat. Wrap bacon slices around the meat and secure with wooden picks. Grill the venison on a preheated grill to desired doneness. Remove to a cutting board and slice.

Citrus-Glazed Baked Ham

Serves 10 to 25

1 (6- to 10-pound) bone-in ham	1/2 teaspoon ground ginger
1 cup orange juice	1/4 teaspoon ground nutmeg
1 (18-ounce) jar orange marmalade	1/4 teaspoon ground cloves
1/2 cup spicy brown mustard	

Place the ham in a large baking pan lined with foil. Combine the orange juice, marmalade, mustard, ginger, nutmeg and cloves in a bowl and mix well. Pour 1 cup over the ham; reserve the remaining glaze. Bake at 350 degrees, on the lowest oven rack, for 12 to 13 minutes per pound, basting once or twice during cooking. Let stand for 15 minutes before carving. Heat the remaining glaze in a saucepan and serve with the ham.

This recipe was contributed by Sweet Magnolia's Tea Bistro.

CITRUS- AND HERB-RUBBED PORK ROAST

6 servings

3 tablespoons extra-virgin olive oil
1 tablespoon finely chopped garlic
3/4 teaspoon freshly ground pepper
1 1/2 teaspoons dried sage
1 1/2 teaspoons dried rosemary
2 teaspoons dried thyme
1 1/2 teaspoons sea salt
1 to 2 teaspoons grated orange zest
1 (2 1/2-pound) boneless pork sirloin roast

Combine the olive oil, garlic, pepper, sage, rosemary, thyme, salt and orange zest in a bowl and mix well. Spread evenly over the entire roast and place in a roasting pan. Roast at 350 degrees for 55 to 75 minutes or to 145 degrees on a meat thermometer. Remove to a platter and cover loosely with foil. Let stand for 15 minutes before slicing.

Variation

This rub may also be used on a rack of lamb or on cubed pork skewers.

PERFECT PORK TENDERLOIN

Serves 4

1 (1-pound) pork tenderloin
1/2 cup olive oil
1/3 cup soy sauce
1/4 cup red wine vinegar
Juice of 1 lemon
2 tablespoons Worcestershire sauce
2 tablespoons fresh parsley, finely
   chopped
2 teaspoons dry mustard

1/2 teaspoon salt
1/2 teaspoon lemon pepper
1/2 teaspoon freshly cracked
   black pepper
4 garlic cloves, minced
1 tablespoon olive oil
1/2 cup chicken broth
2 teaspoons grated lemon zest
2 teaspoons butter

Place the pork in a sealable plastic bag. Whisk 1/2 cup olive oil, soy sauce, vinegar, lemon juice, Worcestershire sauce, parsley, mustard, salt, lemon pepper, black pepper and garlic in a bowl. Remove and reserve 3 tablespoons of the marinade. Pour the remaining marinade over the pork. Seal tightly and turn to coat. Marinate in the refrigerator for 3 hours.

Remove the pork and discard the marinade. Heat 1 tablespoon olive oil in an ovenproof skillet over medium-high heat. Add the pork and sear for 2 to 3 minutes per side. Place in a 350-degree oven and cook for 40 minutes or to 160 degrees on a meat thermometer. Remove the meat to a platter and keep warm.

Add the broth to the skillet and cook, stirring constantly, scraping any browned bits from the bottom of the skillet. Stir in the reserved marinade and lemon zest. Cook for 2 to 3 minutes. Add the butter and remove from the heat. Stir until the butter is melted. Pour over the pork and serve.

SOUTH AFRICAN SPICED PORK KABOBS

Serves 6 to 8

1 tablespoon coarse sea salt
2 teaspoons dried oregano
2 teaspoons fresh rosemary
1 tablespoon caraway seeds
1 teaspoon cumin seeds
1/2 teaspoon ground turmeric
2 tablespoons harissa sauce
1 tablespoon Sriracha sauce (optional)
1 garlic clove, crushed
1/4 cup extra-virgin olive oil
1/2 cup orange juice
4 pounds pork loin, trimmed and cut into 1-inch cubes
2 large red onions, cut into 1-inch pieces
2 large red or yellow bell peppers, cut into 1-inch pieces
16 metal skewers or water-soaked bamboo skewers

Grind the salt, oregano, rosemary, caraway seeds, cumin seeds and turmeric in a spice grinder and remove to a large bowl. Add the harissa sauce, Sriracha sauce, garlic, olive oil and orange juice and mix well. Add the pork and mix well. Remove to two 1-gallon sealable plastic bags and seal tightly. Marinate in the refrigerator for 4 hours to overnight.

Remove the pork and discard the marinade. Thread the pork, onions and bell peppers alternately onto the skewers. Grill over medium heat for 6 minutes per side or until the pork is cooked through. Serve hot with Coconut Rice (page 75) or steamed rice.

Wine Pairing

Serve this dish with a West Coast red zinfandel. These full-bodied red wines are bold and fruity, making them an excellent choice for pairing with this recipe. The tannins in these wines will counter the spices in the dish.

SWEET-AND-SPICY BABY BACK RIBS

Serves 6

3 racks baby back ribs
Olive oil for brushing
2 tablespoons ground cumin
1/4 cup packed brown sugar
1/2 cup paprika
1/4 cup chili powder
2 tablespoons cayenne pepper (optional)
1 teaspoon ground mace
1/4 cup kosher or sea salt
1/4 cup cracked black pepper
2 (12-ounce) cans beer or 4 cups chicken broth
Favorite barbecue sauce (optional)

Rinse the ribs with cold water and pat dry with paper towels. Remove the thin membrane from the back of the ribs. Cut each rack in half, to make six racks of 7 to 8 ribs each. Arrange the ribs on two foil-lined shallow baking pans coated with nonstick cooking spray. Brush the ribs lightly with olive oil. Combine the cumin, brown sugar, paprika, chili powder, cayenne pepper, mace, salt and black pepper in a bowl and mix well. Sprinkle generously over both sides of the ribs and let stand, meat side up, for 30 minutes. Reserve any remaining spice rub for another use.

Bake the ribs at 450 degrees, on the middle and upper oven racks, for 10 minutes. Reduce the heat to 250 degrees and bake for 1 hour. Turn the ribs over. Pour 1 can of beer into each pan and cover tightly with foil. Rotate the pan placement and bake for 1 1/2 hours longer. Remove and let stand for 30 minutes. Cut the racks into 2-rib portions.

Grill over medium heat, brushing with barbecue sauce. You may also chill the ribs overnight before grilling. Bring to room temperature and heat on the grill or bake at 350 degrees for 15 minutes.

BAKED JAMBALAYA

Serves 4 to 6

2 tablespoons butter or olive oil
1 cup finely chopped onion
1/2 cup finely chopped green bell pepper
2 garlic cloves, minced
1 1/2 cups chopped cooked chicken
1 cup chopped cooked ham
8 ounces smoked sausage, cut into 1/4-inch slices
1 (15-ounce) can crushed tomatoes
1 cup rice
1 1/2 cups low-sodium chicken broth
1/2 teaspoon dried thyme
1/2 teaspoon chili powder
1 1/2 teaspoons salt
1/4 teaspoon freshly ground pepper
1 tablespoon chopped fresh parsley

Melt the butter in a Dutch oven over medium-high heat. Add the onion, bell pepper and garlic and sauté until the vegetables are tender. Stir in the chicken, ham and sausage. Cook for 5 minutes, stirring constantly. Stir in the tomatoes, rice, broth, thyme, chili powder, salt and pepper and remove from the heat. Bake, covered, at 350 degrees for 1 1/4 hours or until the rice is tender. Spoon onto serving plates and sprinkle with the parsley.

Baked Monte Cristo Sandwiches

Serves 6

2 (8-count) cans refrigerator crescent rolls
2 tablespoons butter or margarine, melted
2 tablespoons honey
6 ounces thinly sliced cooked turkey
6 ounces thinly sliced ham
6 ounces sliced Muenster cheese
1/3 to 1/2 cup red raspberry preserves
2 tablespoons honey

For the crescent roll, unroll the dough. Separate into 4 rectangles, pressing the perforations to seal. Arrange the rectangles, without touching, on a baking sheet coated with nonstick cooking spray.

Mix the melted butter and 2 tablespoons honey in a bowl and brush over the rectangles. Bake at 375 degrees for 8 to 12 minutes or just until beginning to brown. Let cool for 15 minutes.

To make the sandwiches, remove one rectangle to a shallow baking pan coated with nonstick cooking spray. Top with the turkey and the second rectangle. Top with the ham and cheese and the third rectangle. Spread the preserves over the rectangle, leaving a small border. Top with the fourth rectangle and brush with 2 tablespoons honey. Bake at 375 degrees for 10 to 15 minutes or until the top is golden brown and the cheese is melted. Cut into squares.

HOLIDAY DISHES

LOCAL RESTAURANTS

In the "Boom Days" of the 1920s, Bertha Hinshaw moved with her husband to Lake Wales to be near her aging parents. The Hinshaws traveled and entertained a great deal, so Bertha, a determined and gutsy lady, decided to make a living for her family doing what she knew best, making people feel at home. Chalet Suzanne, named for the Hinshaws' only daughter, opened its doors in 1931.

Four generations of the Hinshaw family have carried on the tradition of the Chalet's cuisine. Guests can enjoy the signature Romaine soup and broiled grapefruit served in one of five quaint rooms, each on a different level, overlooking the lake. Every corner glows with antiques, stained glass, and old lamps.

Fast forward almost ninety years, and there is a similar dream coming true in Central Florida. After moving from Italy to Switzerland to attend culinary school and working in restaurants throughout Europe, Chef Franco Basalone came to America with his beautiful bride, Cynthia, who wanted to be close to her hometown of Lakeland. Chef Basalone worked in a local restaurant before deciding to create his own in a comfortable and beautiful location. Arabellas Ristorante is a cozy Italian restaurant located in a corner spot in downtown Winter Haven. He then expanded his dream next door to include the informal Bistro Pizza and the upscale Ave. Bar. His family of restaurants will soon expand to include a premier upscale steakhouse.

White Christmas Cocktail

Serves 4 to 6

1 pint vanilla ice cream, softened
1 cup heavy whipping cream
2 cups brewed coffee
1/4 cup sugar

6 to 9 ounces caramel-flavored
   Irish cream liqueur
Cinnamon

Combine the ice cream, cream, coffee and sugar in a pitcher and stir until the ice cream is melted. Pour 1 1/2 ounces of liqueur into each chilled old-fashioned glass and fill with the coffee mixture. Sprinkle with cinnamon.

Warm Spiced Toddies

Serves 6

32 ounces cranberry juice cocktail
32 ounces pomegranate juice
3 cinnamon sticks
1 (1-inch) piece fresh ginger,
   peeled and sliced
1 1/2 cups gold rum
Juice of 2 limes

Heat the cranberry juice cocktail, pomegranate juice, cinnamon sticks and ginger in a saucepan to a simmer. Cook, covered, over low heat for 30 minutes. Remove and discard the cinnamon sticks and ginger. Stir in the rum and lime juice and serve immediately.

HOT BUTTERED RUM

Serves 4

1/2 cup (1 stick) butter, softened
2/3 cup packed dark brown sugar
1 teaspoon grated orange zest
1 teaspoon vanilla extract
3/4 teaspoon cinnamon
3/4 teaspoon ginger
1/2 teaspoon nutmeg
3/4 cup dark rum
3 cups boiling water

Beat the butter, brown sugar, orange zest, vanilla, cinnamon, ginger and nutmeg in a mixing bowl at medium speed for 1 minute to mix well. Add 2 tablespoons butter mixture and 3 tablespoons rum to each of four heatproof glasses. Add 3/4 cup boiling water to each glass and stir to mix.

Citrus Zest

When a recipe calls for citrus juice, check to see if it also calls for citrus zest. If so, zest the fruit before juicing it.

Praline-Mandarin Endive

Serves 15

2 heads Belgian endive
1/2 cup crumbled blue cheese
1 cup drained canned mandarin oranges
1/2 cup crumbled pralines
3 tablespoons balsamic vinegar

Arrange the individual leaves of endive on a serving platter. Fill the leaves with equal portions of the cheese, oranges and pralines. Drizzle with the vinegar and serve.

Pesto Tomatoes

Serves 16

2 cups packed fresh basil leaves
2 garlic cloves
1/4 cup pine nuts
2/3 cup extra-virgin olive oil
Kosher salt and freshly ground pepper
*   to taste*

1/2 cup (2 ounces) freshly grated
*   pecorino cheese*
16 cherry tomatoes
2 tablespoons grated Parmesan
*   cheese*

Pulse the basil, garlic and pine nuts in a food processor until coarsely chopped. Add three-fourths of the olive oil and process until smooth. Season with salt and pepper and add the remaining olive oil. Pulse to mix well. Remove to a bowl and stir in the pecorino cheese. Reserve 1/2 cup of pesto sauce to fill the tomatoes and save the remainder for another use. Cut the top off the tomatoes and scoop out the center, leaving a shell. Fill each tomato shell with pesto. Sprinkle the tomatoes with the Parmesan cheese.

CRAB CAKES WITH SMOKY CITRUS DRIZZLE

Serves 4

1 tablespoon olive oil
1/2 onion, finely chopped
2 garlic cloves, minced
1 pound jumbo lump crab meat, shells
   removed
1 cup fresh white bread crumbs
1 tablespoon (or more) mayonnaise
1 egg white

2 tablespoons lime juice
2 tablespoons chopped cilantro
Sea salt and pepper to taste
1 cup blue or yellow cornmeal
4 1/2 teaspoons olive oil
Smoky Citrus Drizzle (below)
Chopped cilantro for garnish

Heat 1 tablespoon olive oil in a skillet over medium heat. Add the onion and garlic and sauté for 5 to 7 minutes or until the onion is caramelized. Remove to a bowl and fold in the crab meat, bread crumbs, mayonnaise, egg white, lime juice, 2 tablespoons cilantro, salt and pepper just until mixed. Shape into four to six crab cakes and place on a plate. Chill, covered, for 30 minutes. Coat the crab cakes in the cornmeal, tapping off any excess. Chill for 30 minutes.

Heat 4 1/2 teaspoons olive oil in a skillet over medium heat. Add the crab cakes and cook for 2 to 3 minutes per side or until golden brown and crisp. Remove to serving plates. Drizzle with the Smoky Citrus Drizzle and serve with Mango-Serrano Relish (page 80) or your choice of side dish. Garnish with additional chopped cilantro.

SMOKY CITRUS DRIZZLE

1/2 cup mayonnaise
1/4 cup sour cream
1/4 teaspoon puréed canned chipotle
   chiles in adobo sauce

Grated zest and juice of 1 lime
1/2 teaspoon honey
Sea salt and pepper to taste

Whisk the mayonnaise, sour cream, chipotle chile, lime zest, lime juice and honey in a bowl. Whisk in a small amount of water to thin, if needed. Season with salt and pepper. Chill until ready to serve.

ZESTY GREEN BEAN BUNDLES

Serves 8

1 pound fresh green beans, washed, dried and trimmed
10 slices maple bacon, cut in half
1/2 cup (1 stick) butter or margarine
1/4 cup packed brown sugar
2 garlic cloves, minced
1/4 teaspoon salt
1/4 teaspoon pepper
Grated orange zest to taste

Wrap 6 to 8 beans with 1 piece of the bacon and lay, seam side down, in a 9×13-inch baking dish. Repeat with the remaining beans and bacon. Melt the butter in a saucepan over medium heat. Stir in the brown sugar, garlic, salt, pepper and orange zest. Pour evenly over the beans and cover with foil. Bake at 350 degrees for 30 minutes. Remove the foil and bake for 15 minutes longer or until the bacon is cooked through and the beans are tender.

Quick Clean-Up

Use a small bowl on the counter top for scraps or garbage so you are not always bending over to throw things away.

TWICE-BAKED POTATOES

Serves 6

6 baking potatoes
1 bunch green onions, chopped
1 cup sour cream
1 cup (4 ounces) shredded Cheddar cheese

Wash the potatoes and prick with a fork. Bake the potatoes at 350 degrees for 1 hour or microwave on High for 15 minutes or until tender. Let the potatoes cool to room temperature. Cut the potatoes in half lengthwise and scoop the pulp into a mixing bowl, leaving 1/2-inch shells. Add the green onions, sour cream and most of the cheese and beat with a hand mixer until the potatoes are smooth. Spoon into the potato shells and sprinkle with the remaining cheese. Place in a shallow baking pan. Bake at 350 degrees for 20 minutes.

BLUE CHEESE RICE

Serves 6 to 8

3 to 4 cups cooked white rice
1 tablespoon fresh lime juice
2 tablespoons melted butter
1/2 teaspoon dry mustard
2 tablespoons dry sherry
4 to 5 green onions, finely chopped

3 hard-cooked eggs, chopped
1 cup reduced-fat sour cream
1 cup pitted black olives, sliced
4 ounces blue cheese, crumbled
Paprika

Combine the rice, lime juice, melted butter, mustard and sherry in a bowl and mix well. Add the green onions, eggs, sour cream and olives and mix gently. Add the cheese and toss gently. Spoon into a lightly greased 1 1/2-quart baking dish. Bake at 350 degrees for 30 minutes. Sprinkle with paprika and serve.

Holiday Beef Tenderloin

Serves 8

1 1/2 cups dry red wine
1 garlic clove, minced
1 (2 1/2- to 3-pound) center-cut beef tenderloin
2 tablespoons mixed peppercorns, coarsely ground
1/2 teaspoon sea salt
1/2 teaspoon crushed red pepper
2 tablespoons dry bread crumbs
2 tablespoons finely chopped fresh parsley
Horseradish Sauce (below)

Add the wine and garlic to a sealable plastic bag. Add the beef, seal tightly and turn to coat. Marinate in the refrigerator for 1 hour. Remove the meat to a rack in a roasting pan and discard the marinade. Combine the peppercorns, salt, red pepper, bread crumbs and parsley in a bowl and mix well. Spread evenly over the beef. Roast at 400 degrees for 30 minutes. Increase the heat to 425 degrees and roast for 15 minutes or to 130 degrees on a meat thermometer for medium-rare. Remove the meat to a platter and cover. Let stand for 15 minutes. Slice and serve with Horseradish Sauce.

Horseradish Sauce

1 cup fat-free sour cream
2 tablespoons prepared horseradish
1 1/2 teaspoons grated lemon zest
1/2 teaspoon Worcestershire sauce
1/4 teaspoon salt

Combine the sour cream, horseradish, lemon zest, Worcestershire sauce and salt in a bowl and mix well.

TRIPLE-CHEESE LASAGNA ROLLS

Serves 6

2 tablespoons unsalted butter

4 teaspoons all-purpose flour

1¼ cups milk

½ teaspoon nutmeg

¼ teaspoon salt

¼ teaspoon pepper

2 tablespoons olive oil

12 uncooked lasagna noodles

Salt

15 ounces whole milk ricotta cheese

1 (10-ounce) package frozen chopped
spinach, thawed and squeezed dry

1 cup (4 ounces) grated Parmesan
cheese

3 ounces thinly sliced prosciutto,
chopped

1 egg, beaten

¾ teaspoon salt

½ teaspoon freshly ground pepper

2 cups marinara sauce

1½ cups (6 ounces) shredded
mozzarella cheese

3 tablespoons grated Parmesan cheese

Melt the butter in a saucepan over medium-low heat. Whisk in the flour and cook for
3 minutes, whisking constantly. Whisk in the milk and increase the heat to medium-high.
Cook for 3 minutes or until thickened and smooth, whisking constantly. Whisk in the nutmeg,
¼ teaspoon salt and ¼ teaspoon pepper. Pour evenly into a buttered 9×13-inch baking
dish. Add the olive oil to a large saucepan of boiling salted water. Add the lasagna
noodles and cook according to package directions; drain. Lay the noodles in a single layer
on a work surface. Combine the ricotta cheese, spinach, 1 cup Parmesan cheese,
prosciutto, egg, ¾ teaspoon salt and ½ teaspoon pepper in a bowl and mix well.
Spread about 3 tablespoons of the cheese mixture over each lasagna noodle and roll up.

Arrange the rolls, seam side down, over the sauce in the baking dish, making certain
the rolls do not touch. Pour one-half of the marinara sauce evenly over the rolls and top with
the mozzarella cheese. Sprinkle with 3 tablespoons Parmesan cheese. Bake, covered, at
450 degrees for 20 minutes. Uncover and bake for 15 minutes longer. Heat the remaining
marinara sauce and serve on the side.

BUTTERNUT RAVIOLI WITH BOURBON-PECAN SAUCE

Serves 6

2 cups cubed butternut squash
1 (14-ounce) can vegetable broth
1 cup ricotta cheese
1/4 cup ground pecans, toasted
1 teaspoon garlic powder
1/2 teaspoon salt

1/4 teaspoon pepper
32 wonton wrappers
Bourbon-Pecan Sauce (below)
Finely chopped fresh parsley for garnish
Chopped pecans for garnish

Bring the squash and broth to a boil in a saucepan. Reduce the heat and cover. Simmer for 15 to 20 minutes or until the squash is tender; drain. Remove the squash to a bowl and mash. Let cool to room temperature. Mix the cheese, pecans, garlic powder, salt and pepper in a bowl. Add to the squash and mix well. Remove one wonton wrapper at a time, covering the others with a damp towel to avoid drying out. Spoon 1 tablespoon of the squash mixture onto the wrapper, slightly off-center. Moisten the edges of the wrapper with water. Fold the wrapper diagonally over the filling and seal the edges with a fork. Repeat to use the remaining wrappers and filling. Chill for 5 to 10 minutes. Bring a large saucepan of water to a boil and reduce to a gentle simmer. Cook the ravioli in batches for 1 to 2 minutes or until they float. Remove with a slotted spoon and keep warm. Serve the ravioli topped with Bourbon-Pecan Sauce and garnished with finely chopped fresh parsley and chopped pecans.

BOURBON-PECAN SAUCE

2 tablespoons butter
2 tablespoons all-purpose flour
1/2 teaspoon salt
1/2 teaspoon pepper

3/4 cup half-and-half
2/3 cup 2% milk
1/2 cup finely chopped pecans, toasted
1 tablespoon bourbon

Melt the butter in a saucepan. Stir in the flour, salt and pepper. Cook for a few minutes, stirring constantly. Stir in the half-and-half and milk gradually. Bring to a boil and cook for 2 minutes or until thickened, stirring constantly. Stir in the pecans and bourbon and cook until heated through.

CHOCOLATE-ORANGE LAVA CAKES WITH MASCARPONE WHIPPED CREAM

Serves 6

6 tablespoons unsalted butter
8 ounces Lindt Intense Orange dark chocolate, chopped
1 tablespoon Grand Marnier
1/3 cup granulated sugar
3 tablespoons all-purpose flour
1/4 teaspoon salt
4 eggs
1/4 cup mascarpone cheese, softened
1/2 cup heavy whipping cream
2 tablespoon confectioners' sugar

For the Lava Cakes: Melt the butter and chocolate in the top of a double boiler over simmering water, stirring frequently. Remove from over the simmering water and stir in the Grand Marnier. Sift in the granulated sugar, flour and salt and mix well. Add the eggs, one at a time, beating well after each addition with a hand mixer. Beat for 3 minutes or to a lighter shade of brown. Fill each of six greased ramekins with 1/3 cup of batter. Chill for 20 minutes to overnight. Arrange the ramekins in a shallow baking pan. Bake at 400 degrees for 8 to10 minutes or just until the top is set but the center is slightly wobbly. Let cool slightly.

For the Mascarpone Whipped Cream: Beat the cheese, cream and confectioners' sugar in a bowl until soft peaks form. Use immediately or chill until ready to serve with the lava cakes.

NAUGHTY SANTA CAKE

Serves 10 to 12

1 cup chopped pecans
1 (2-layer) package yellow cake mix
2 eggs
1 cup rum, whiskey or bourbon
1/3 cup water
1/2 cup applesauce
3/4 cup fresh orange juice
1/4 cup rum, whiskey or bourbon
2 cups confectioners' sugar

For the cake: Sprinkle the pecans evenly over the bottom of a greased 9×13-inch baking dish. Beat the cake mix, eggs, 1 cup rum, water and applesauce in a mixing bowl at low speed until moistened. Beat at medium speed for 2 to 3 minutes. Pour over the pecans. Bake at 350 degrees for 30 to 40 minutes or until a wooden pick inserted in the center comes out clean. Cool in the pan for 10 minutes. Invert the cake onto a serving platter.

For the glaze: Heat the orange juice and 1/4 cup rum in a saucepan over medium heat. Stir in the confectioners' sugar gradually. Cook until the sugar is dissolved, stirring constantly. Poke holes over the top of the cake with a wooden pick or fork. Pour the glaze evenly over the cake and allow to soak in before serving.

Wine Pairing

Chardonnay, a full-bodied wine with buttery flavors and hints of oak, pairs well with the hints of cocoa in this moist, light, and fluffy Red Velvet Cake (at right).

RED VELVET CAKE

Serves 15

1/2 cup (1 stick) butter, softened
1 1/2 cups sugar
2 eggs, at room temperature
2 teaspoons baking cocoa
2 (1-ounce) bottles red food color
2 1/2 cups cake flour

1 teaspoon salt
1 cup buttermilk
1 teaspoon vanilla extract
1 teaspoon vinegar
1 teaspoon baking soda
Boiled Icing (below)

Beat the butter in a mixing bowl until smooth. Add the sugar and eggs and beat until light and fluffy. Mix the baking cocoa and food color in a small bowl and beat into the butter mixture. Mix the flour and salt together. Beat into the batter alternately with the buttermilk. Beat in the vanilla. Mix the vinegar and baking soda together in a small bowl. Beat into the batter at low speed just until blended. Pour into three nonstick 9-inch cake pans. Bake at 350 degrees for 30 minutes or until the cake tests done. Cool in the pan for 10 minutes. Remove to a wire rack to cool completely. Frost the cooled cake with the Boiled Icing.

BOILED ICING

7 1/2 tablespoons all-purpose flour
1 tablespoon sugar
1 1/2 cups milk

1 1/2 cups sugar
1 1/2 cups (3 sticks) butter, softened
1 1/2 teaspoons vanilla extract

Mix the flour and 1 tablespoon sugar in a saucepan. Whisk in the milk. Cook over medium heat until thick, whisking constantly. Remove from the heat and let cool. Beat 1 1/2 cups sugar, butter and vanilla in a mixing bowl for 15 minutes or until very light and fluffy. Beat in the flour mixture by teaspoonfuls and beat until the consistency of whipped cream.

DESSERTS

"Shopping is a Pleasure" Began in Winter Haven

The Publix legacy started right here in 1930 when 22-year-old George Jenkins opened his first Publix Food Store on Fourth Street NW in downtown Winter Haven. The building facing Central Park still stands today and is home to Scores restaurant. Jenkins worked at the Piggly Wiggly Store and had ideas to grow the business, but after traveling to Atlanta to discuss the concepts and not getting an audience, he returned and opened his own store next door. One story has it that the Piggly Wiggly had scales that required customers to pay a penny to learn their weight. Jenkins installed a scale that would weigh the customer for free—a tradition that continues to this day.

In 1940, Jenkins moved his store several blocks east and Publix opened Florida's first supermarket. This "food palace" was made of marble, glass, and stucco and was equipped with innovations never seen before in a grocery store. It featured air conditioning, fluorescent lighting, electric-eye doors, frozen food cases, and background music. There were eight-foot-wide aisles and open dairy cases designed to custom specifications. The store also had in-store doughnut and flower shops. People traveled for miles to shop there, and many local residents remember playing with the automatic doors or watching the doughnuts being made when they stopped in on their way home from school.

The "food palace" still stands facing Central Avenue at Second Street NW. It functioned as Publix #1 until 1957, when the company opened the Northgate Shopping Center.

From that first store and six employees, Publix has grown into a Fortune 500 company with 1,068 locations and 156,000 employees.* Winter Haven is proud of its role as the birthplace of Publix Super Markets.

*Source: www.publix.com

SOUR CREAM POUND CAKE WITH CITRUS GLAZE

Serves 10 to 12

1 cup (2 sticks) butter, softened
3 cups sugar
6 eggs
3 cups cake flour

1/4 teaspoon baking soda
1 cup sour cream
2 teaspoons vanilla extract
Citrus Glaze (below)

Beat the butter and sugar in a mixing bowl until light and fluffy. Add the eggs, one at a time, beating well after each addition. Beat in the flour and baking soda. Add the sour cream and vanilla and beat well. Pour into a nonstick bundt pan or tube pan.

Place in a preheated 500-degree oven and immediately reduce the heat to 300 degrees. Bake for 1 1/2 hours or until the cake tests done. Cool in the pan for 10 minutes. Remove to a wire rack to cool completely. Pour the Citrus Glaze evenly over the cooled cake.

CITRUS GLAZE

3/4 cup confectioners' sugar
1/4 cup orange juice
1 teaspoon vanilla extract
1 teaspoon almond extract

Combine the confectioners' sugar, orange juice, vanilla and almond extract in a bowl and mix until smooth.

Orange Aspic Pound Cake

Serves 8

1 (13-ounce) can Chalet Suzanne Orange Aspic
1 (2-layer) package yellow cake mix
1 (4-ounce) package vanilla instant pudding mix
4 eggs, beaten
2/3 cup water
1/4 cup vegetable oil
1 tablespoon butter
2 cups confectioners' sugar

For the cake: Add 1 cup of the orange aspic to a mixing bowl and reserve the remainder for the glaze. Add the cake mix, pudding mix, eggs, water and oil to the mixing bowl and beat at low speed until moistened. Beat at medium speed for 2 minutes. Pour into a greased and floured 9-inch bundt pan. Bake at 325 degrees for 45 minutes or until a wooden pick inserted in the center comes out clean. Cool in the pan for 10 to 15 minutes. Remove to a cake plate to cool completely.

For the glaze: Cook the remainder of the orange aspic in a saucepan until thinned. Add the butter and cook until the butter is melted, stirring frequently. Add the confectioners' sugar and stir until blended. Drizzle over the cooled cake.

This recipe was contributed by the Chalet Suzanne Restaurant & Inn.

Read the Recipe First

Read every recipe thoroughly before prepping the ingredients.

CARROT CAKE WITH PINEAPPLE CREAM CHEESE FROSTING

Serves 16

2 cups all-purpose flour
2 cups sugar
2 teaspoons baking soda
2 teaspoons cinnamon
1 teaspoon salt
3 eggs
1 1/2 cups vegetable oil

2 teaspoons vanilla extract
2 cups grated carrots
1/2 cup crushed pineapple, drained
1/2 cup nuts, chopped (optional)
Pineapple Cream Cheese Frosting (below)

Mix the flour, sugar, baking soda, cinnamon and salt in a large bowl. Add the eggs, oil, vanilla, carrots, pineapple and nuts and mix well. Pour into a greased and floured 9×13-inch baking pan. Bake at 350 degrees for 1 hour or until the cake tests done. Remove to a wire rack to cool completely before frosting with the Pineapple Cream Cheese Frosting.

PINEAPPLE CREAM CHEESE FROSTING

1/2 cup (1 stick) butter, softened
3 ounces cream cheese, softened
2 cups confectioners' sugar
2 tablespoons crushed pineapple, drained
1/4 cup finely chopped nuts

Beat the butter, cream cheese and confectioners' sugar in a bowl until light and fluffy. Stir in the pineapple and nuts.

PINK LEMONADE CAKE

Serves 10

1 (2-layer) package lemon cake mix
1 (4-ounce) package lemon instant pudding mix
4 eggs
1/3 cup vegetable oil
1/2 cup milk
1/2 cup pink lemonade concentrate, thawed
3 to 4 drops pink food color
Pink Lemonade Glaze (below)

Combine the cake mix, pudding mix, eggs, oil, milk and lemonade concentrate in a bowl and mix until smooth. Stir in food color to reach desired color. Pour into a greased and floured bundt pan. Bake at 350 degrees for 1 hour or until the cake tests done. Cool in the pan for 10 to 15 minutes. Remove to a wire rack to cool completely. Spread the Pink Lemonade Glaze over the cooled cake. Save any remaining glaze for another use.

PINK LEMONADE GLAZE

1 cup (2 sticks) unsalted butter, softened
6 cups (or less) confectioners' sugar
1/2 cup pink lemonade concentrate,
    thawed
3 to 4 drops pink food color
Grated lemon zest to taste

Mix the butter with 3 cups of the confectioners' sugar in a bowl. Add the lemonade concentrate and mix well. Stir in enough of the remaining confectioners' sugar to reach a spreading consistency. Stir in food color to reach desired color. Stir in lemon zest. Remove to a saucepan and heat until the frosting thins slightly or microwave in a microwave-safe bowl at short intervals to thin slightly.

CHAMPAGNE CAKE POPS

Makes 4 dozen cake pops

3 cups cake flour
1 1/2 teaspoons baking powder
1 teaspoon baking soda
1 teaspoon salt
2 cups Champagne, at room
   temperature
2 teaspoons vanilla extract
3/4 cup (1 1/2 sticks) unsalted butter,
   softened

1 3/4 cups sugar
6 egg whites, at room temperature
Champagne Buttercream Icing
   (page 131)
Chocolate almond bark
48 white lollipop sticks
Edible gold glitter

Mix the flour, baking powder, baking soda and salt together. Mix the Champagne and vanilla in a bowl. Beat the butter and sugar in a mixing bowl at medium speed until light and fluffy. Beat in the egg whites gradually at medium speed. Beat in the dry ingredients alternately with the Champagne mixture, beginning and ending with the dry ingredients; do not overmix. Pour into two greased and floured 8×8-inch baking pans. Bake at 350 degrees for 30 minutes or until a wooden pick inserted in the center comes out clean. Remove to a wire rack to cool completely.

Break up each pan of cooled cake in a separate mixing bowl at slow speed. Beat 1 cup of the Champagne Buttercream Icing into each. Shape into balls and arrange on a parchment-lined baking sheet. Chill for 30 minutes.

Microwave a small amount of chocolate bark in a microwave-safe bowl at short intervals until melted. Dip one end of each lollipop stick into the melted chocolate and insert into one cake ball. Return to the parchment-lined baking sheet. Repeat to use all of the cake balls and lollipop sticks. Chill for 30 minutes.

Microwave the remaining chocolate bark in a microwave-safe bowl at short intervals until melted. Coat each cake ball in melted chocolate and return to the parchment-lined baking sheet. Sprinkle with gold glitter and let stand until the chocolate coating is set. Store in an airtight container.

CHAMPAGNE BUTTERCREAM ICING

1 1/2 cups (3 sticks) plus 2 tablespoons unsalted butter, softened
3 cups sifted confectioners' sugar
1/8 teaspoon salt
2 teaspoons vanilla extract
1/4 cup Champagne, at room temperature

Beat the butter in a mixing bowl at medium speed until light and fluffy. Beat in the confectioners' sugar gradually and beat at medium speed for 5 minutes. Add the salt, vanilla and Champagne and beat at medium speed for 3 minutes.

SALTED PECAN PIE

Serves 8

1 unbaked frozen deep-dish pie shell
1 cup packed light brown sugar
1 cup dark corn syrup
6 tablespoons unsalted butter,
* cut into pieces*

1 tablespoon coarse sea salt
3 eggs, beaten
2 cups chopped pecans
Sea salt for garnish

Place the pie shell on a foil-lined baking sheet and prick with a fork. Bake at 350 degrees for 15 minutes. Mix the brown sugar, corn syrup, butter and salt in a saucepan. Cook over medium heat until the butter is melted, stirring frequently. Remove from the heat and cool to room temperature. Whisk in the eggs and stir in the pecans. Pour into the pie shell. Bake at 350 degrees for 45 to 50 minutes or until the center is set. Remove to a wire rack to cool completely. Garnish each slice with a sprinkle of sea salt.

Wine Pairing

Pair this not so achingly sweet but intense dessert experience with a nice medium-dry tawny port. The nutty flavors of the port will pair well with the pie.

KEY LIME TARTLETS

Serves 12

4 egg yolks
1 (14-ounce) can sweetened condensed milk
1/2 cup Key lime juice
12 mini graham cracker pie shells
Whipped cream for garnish

Combine the egg yolks, sweetened condensed milk and lime juice in a bowl and mix well. Pour into the pie shells. Chill for several hours. Garnish with whipped cream and serve.

Note: If you are concerned about using raw egg yolks, use yolks from eggs pasteurized in their shells, which are sold at some specialty food stores, or use an equivalent amount of pasteurized egg substitute.

Citrus Zest—A Cook's Secret

If you are making a recipe that calls only for the juice of a citrus fruit, you can finely zest the fruit before you juice it. Divide the zest into one-teaspoon increments and wrap each tightly in plastic wrap, squeezing to remove all the air. Place in a plastic freezer bag labeled with the date, and store in the freezer for up to three months.

WHISKEY BREAD PUDDING

Serves 8 to 10

2 eggs
3 tablespoons butter, melted
2 tablespoons vanilla extract
2 1/2 cups milk
2 cups sugar

2 heaping cups small sourdough
  bread cubes
1/2 cup pecans, chopped
Whiskey Sauce (below)

Whisk the eggs in a bowl. Whisk in the melted butter, vanilla and milk. Whisk in the sugar gradually; whisk until the sugar is dissolved. Toss the bread with the pecans in a bowl and spread in a 9 × 9-inch baking dish. Pour the egg mixture evenly over the bread. Bake at 325 degrees for 1 hour or until golden brown. Top with the hot Whiskey Sauce and serve immediately.

WHISKEY SAUCE

1/2 cup sugar
1/2 cup (1 stick) butter
1/2 cup heavy cream
1/4 cup whiskey

Combine the sugar, butter, cream and whiskey in a saucepan. Cook over low heat to a gentle boil, stirring constantly. Serve immediately.

APPLE CRISP

Serves 8 to 10

4 cups sliced peeled apples
1/4 cup water
1 teaspoon cinnamon
1/2 teaspoon salt

1 cup sugar
3/4 cup all-purpose flour
5 1/3 tablespoons cold butter,
   cut into small pieces

Arrange the apples in a baking dish and sprinkle with the water, cinnamon and salt. Mix the sugar and flour in a bowl. Cut in the butter until crumbly. Sprinkle over the apples. Bake at 350 degrees for 45 minutes.

BUTTER COOKIES

Makes 3 dozen cookies

3 cups all-purpose flour
1/2 teaspoon baking powder
1 cup (2 sticks) butter, softened

1/2 cup sugar
1 egg
1 tablespoon vanilla extract

Mix the flour and baking powder together. Beat the butter and sugar in a mixing bowl until light and fluffy. Beat in the egg and vanilla. Beat in the dry ingredients just until a dough forms; do not overmix. Chill, covered, for several hours. Roll 1/4 inch thick on a floured surface. Cut with a cookie cutter and arrange on a cookie sheet. Bake at 425 degrees for 5 to 7 minutes or until lightly browned. Cool on the cookie sheet for 2 minutes. Remove to a wire rack to cool completely. Frost and decorate when cool, if desired.

Heavenly Chocolate-Pecan Bars

Makes 30 bars

1/2 cup (1 stick) butter, softened
1 cup all-purpose flour
1/4 cup sugar
1 cup graham cracker crumbs
1 teaspoon baking powder
1/4 teaspoon salt

1/2 cup chocolate chips
1 (14-ounce) can sweetened
    condensed milk
1/2 cup pecans (optional)
Buttercream Frosting (below)

Combine the butter, flour and sugar in a bowl and mix well. Press evenly into a 9×13-inch baking dish, using waxed paper against the crust to keep fingers from sticking. Bake at 350 degrees for 10 minutes or bake longer for a crisper crust. Remove to a wire rack to cool for at least 10 minutes.

Mix the graham cracker crumbs, baking powder and salt in a bowl. Add the chocolate chips, sweetened condensed milk and pecans and mix well. Spread carefully over the partially baked crust. Bake at 350 degrees for 15 to 20 minutes or until golden brown or bake longer for a toffee-like filling. Remove to a wire rack to cool completely. Spread the Buttercream Frosting over the cooled filling and cut into bars.

Buttercream Frosting

1 1/2 cups confectioners' sugar
1/2 cup (1 stick) butter, softened
1 teaspoon vanilla extract

1 cup half-and-half
Milk

Combine the confectioners' sugar, butter, vanilla and half-and-half in a bowl and mix until smooth. Stir in a small amount of milk if needed for a creamy consistency.

Girls' Night Out Bourbon Balls

Makes 4 dozen bourbon balls

1/2 cup (1 stick) butter, softened
3 1/4 cups confectioners' sugar
1/4 cup bourbon
1/2 cup chopped pecans
2 cups semisweet chocolate chips
2 ounces (1/2 slab) paraffin

For the bourbon balls: Beat the butter, confectioners' sugar and bourbon in a bowl until smooth. Stir in the pecans. Shape into 1-inch balls and chill for 1 1/2 hours.

For the chocolate coating: Melt the chocolate chips and paraffin in the top of a double boiler over simmering water, stirring constantly, or microwave in a microwave-safe bowl at short intervals to melt.

Insert a wooden pick into a bourbon ball and dip into the chocolate mixture to coat. Shake off excess chocolate gently and place on waxed paper. Repeat with the remaining bourbon balls and melted chocolate. Let stand until set. Store in an airtight container in the refrigerator.

Parchment Paper

Parchment paper can be your best friend. Be sure to line baking sheets and cake pans with it for easy clean-up.

CARAMEL CASHEW CLUSTERS

Makes 3 dozen clusters

2 cups coarsely chopped cashews
2 ounces German's sweet chocolate
1 cup milk chocolate chips
16 ounces white almond bark

1 cup unwrapped caramels
1 tablespoon milk
Coarse sea salt

Layer the cashews, sweet chocolate, milk chocolate chips and almond bark in a slow cooker in the order listed. Cook, covered, on Low for 2 1/2 hours; do not remove the lid during cooking. Stir at the end of cooking to mix well. Drop by teaspoonfuls onto a waxed-paper lined baking sheet. Cook the caramels and milk in a saucepan over low heat until the caramels are melted, stirring frequently. Drizzle the caramel over the clusters and sprinkle with sea salt. Chill until set. Store in an airtight container.

CORNFLAKE KISSES

Makes 2 dozen cookies

2 egg whites
1 cup confectioners' sugar
2 teaspoons vanilla extract

2 1/2 cups cornflakes
1 cup chopped pecans

Beat the egg whites in a mixing bowl until stiff peaks form. Beat in the confectioners' sugar and vanilla. Stir in the cornflakes and pecans. Drop by large spoonfuls onto a parchment-lined cookie sheet. Bake at 300 degrees for 30 minutes or until firm. Let cool on the cookie sheet for 2 minutes. Remove to a wire rack to cool completely.

COOKBOOK COMMITTEE

Jae Lynn Akin	Holly Hughes	Jennifer Myers	Martha Seney
Jill Bentley	Mary Beth Jackson	Mandy O'Halloran	Julie Smith
Melissa Burns	Allison Lee	Renee Pobjecky	Lisa Weathersbee

COOKBOOK CONTRIBUTORS

Thank you to everyone who put in countless hours contributing recipes and testing recipes. The JLGWH greatly appreciates all of your hard work and dedication. We have made every effort to express our many thanks to all the people who have made this project possible. You have our sincerest apologies if your name has been overlooked.

Jae Lynn Akin	Megan Gillis	Wendy Morris	Martha Seney
Joy Barranco	Kathy Girouard	Jennifer Myers	Donna Sheehan
Katie Campbell Barris	Brandy Gray	Linda Myers	Claire Simmons
Cindy Baxter	Daphne Gray	PJ Myers	Dianne Smith
Lou Bell	Lia Gray	Heather Nedley	Julie Smith
Jill Bentley	Christi Holby	Angela Newell	Mary Ann Snively
Heather Bogdahn	Holly Hughes	Amanda O'Halloran	Suzann Threadgill
Jamie Bonifay	Mark Jackson	Paula Orcutt	Kit Threlkel
Cindy Bruce	Mary Beth Jackson	Jan Phillips	Edie Trinklein
Melissa Burns	Lauren Jones	April Porter	Amy Tucker
Marge Crittenden	Allison Lee	Adrienne Richardson	Sheila Walsh Leavey
Meredith Curtis	Avery LeFils	Pat Roberts	Mary Fran Whittinghill
Jill Dunlop	Dorian McGill	Carol Roe	Susan Williams
Deidre Fontenot	Elizabeth McWhorter	Elsie Savant	
Laura Frost	Amy Miles	Jennifer Schaal	

INDEX

Junior League of Greater Winter Haven
P.O. Box 7161
Winter Haven, Florida 33883-7161
863-583-7659
info@jlgwh.com
www.jlgwh.com

Your Order	Quantity	Total
A Splash of Citrus @ $21.95		
Shipping and handling @ $5.95 for one book; $2.00 each additional book		
	Subtotal	
Florida residents add 7% sales tax		
	Total	

Name _____

Street Address _____

City _____ State _____ Zip _____

Telephone _____ E-mail Address _____

Method of Payment ❏ Visa ❏ Mastercard ❏ Checks payable to JLGWH

Account Number _____ Expiration Date _____

Signature _____

Photocopies will be accepted